EVERYDAY SEEING

EVERYDAY SEEING

daily meditations on the One within

Douglas Harding

Quotations selected by
Richard Lang

THE SHOLLOND TRUST

Published by The Shollond Trust
87B Cazenove Road
London N16 6BB
England
headexchange@gn.apc.org
www.headless.org

Cover design: rangsgraphics.com
Interior design: Richard Lang
Thanks to Judy Bruce for her help.
Thanks to David Lang for permission to
include quotations from *Face To No-Face*.

for
you

PREFACE

It is easy to see Who you are. Simply be aware of the place you are looking out of: this faceless space, this single eye, this wider than wide openness that embraces and is the world, this wondrous source from which all things flow.

But how do we stay awake to this blessing at our centre?

When you love someone, naturally you want to spend time with them. The more time you spend with them, the more adorable they are—and the more you want to be with them.

It's the same with the One within us, 'the soul of our soul'.

These daily meditations are invitations to spend more time with this Beauty, this Wisdom, this Love, this Joy—with the One that is wholly yourself yet wholly other.

Richard Lang

daily meditations

No longer so damned cocksure
I know what it's like being me,
I dare to start all over again
and bow before the evidence:
actually as well as metaphorically.
I bend and bow so deeply
that I come to the very edge of me
and my world,
to the Bottom Line it all arises from.
A frontier that doesn't prevent me
from gazing past it
and in
to the Infinite Source of All,
brilliantly on display
yet awesomely mysterious.

When you consciously become
Who you are anyway
(and accordingly your attitude is
wholly accepting and positive)
will you as a human being turn
out to be less (or more) positive
and creative and energetic,
as you start living from the truth
that intrinsically
you aren't a human being at all?

The answer is:
see Who you are at centre,
and then see what you get up to out there.
Be prepared to tap
undreamed-of energies.

When I turn from what I'm looking at,
to what I'm looking out of,
I see nothing.
Examination of this spot
with a fresh and open mind
reveals not the slightest trace of
eyes, mouth, ears, hair, bone, blood, brain.
Try as I may, I can find here no outline,
no cloud, no tint, however shadowy.
In fact, there never was anything here.
I only imagined it.

Where I'm coming from
is upstream of life.
It is the source of life,
yes,
but it is not alive.
From Here I look out upon a snail
or a daffodil there,
let alone you,
and, my God,
I discover life.

What I look like is your job:
you take care of that.
I'm looking after where it's coming from:
this Awake Mystery,
Space,
Capacity,
Stillness,
Immensity,
visibly in receipt of the world.
It's where I'm coming from.

January 6

I suggest that today, as far as possible,
you leave your appearance to me.
I'll look after it.
I'm very grateful to you for it:
I think it is delightful.
Leave that to me
and attend to where you are coming from,
to what is giving rise to your appearance,
to where you are,
to what you are looking out of.
That is not your appearance:
that is your Reality,
central to you,
and is alleged to be not human at all,
but nothing less than
the Kingdom,
the Power and the Glory
behind this fabulous world.

As Who you really, really are
there's nothing and no-one above you
to boss you
and nothing and no-one below you
to bug you.
If you go on to describe
this twofold liberation
as participation in the divine freedom
of the One
who alone is truly free,
who is Freedom itself,
I'm with you all the way.

Our freedom
does not consist in denying
all that determines us
and asserting our own self-will.
On the contrary,
its true ground is our willingness to accept
every necessity,
so that it ceases to be merely external.
We are free in so far as we join our will to God's.
For He alone is by nature free
because subject to no outside influence;
yet He lets us share this freedom
by uniting ourselves to Him.
We have the choice of His freedom
or our bondage.

There's no escaping the fact that,
to be a man or a woman, a child or an adult,
you have to be infinitely less than that
and infinitely more than that.
No way can you shrug off your mystery
and your grandeur.
No way can you get out of being,
at the end of the day that has no beginning or end,
the Best and the Greatest,
the One and Only.

This Origin of all,
having none of the qualities of its products,
is knowable only by contrast with them, negatively,
as spaceless, timeless, limitless,
unthinkable, ungraspable,
completely baffling.
And, just because it is so stainless and aseptic,
so clean of the brand-marks and limitations and defects
which its creatures are necessarily subject to,
it is their cleansing,
their sovereign remedy,
their only lasting cure.

Just as body and mind
are truly realised and invigorated
by seeing them off from here to there,
so also is Spirit.
All the varieties of religious and mystical experience
one ever enjoyed,
evicted from the central position
they never in fact occupied,
come into their own
as they are restored to the world,
to the manifested universe
which is replete at last with all those qualities,
physical and mental *and spiritual*,
which are its own.
Here can be found none of all that,
but only the clean cool air of…
No, it's better not to try to stick a label
on this surfaceless Abyss.

Here alone
the confrontation which is Humanity's curse
is exposed as *the* lie, and so undermined;
the firm basis
of unsentimental and unconditional love
is laid down;
tranquillity and rocklike steadiness
and the end of fear are assured;
the secret of unfailing inspiration is let out,
along with that of ordinary efficiency
and pleasure in work;
the inexhaustible wealth and liberality
of the real world are suddenly released;
the power and the glory that,
in one's heart of hearts,
one always knew one had,
are found to be indeed
one's very own:
correction, One's very own.

If I'm suffering
from this disease of confrontation
in my relationship with you at this moment,
what's the use of trying to deal
with the same problem of confrontation at other levels:
national and international, confrontation between sexes,
ethnic groups, religions, ideologies, power blocs, and so on?
In other words, service to the world begins at home:
if only because when you've found out
Who you are
you find
you are the world.

JANUARY 14

Truly
it is one of the unforeseen pleasures
of the First Person life
to gaze unabashed into the faces of one's friends,
without feeling or thinking anything in particular,
and just see them for what they always were:
things for looking at
and never for looking out of.
This isn't an unloving state,
reducing you to a cardboard cut-out.
Quite the reverse:
it is a most loving refusal to separate
my Consciousness from yours,
and it removes the last barrier between us.
Liberated from the superstition of plural spirits,
we are at last really one.
This is the perfect love which casts out fear:
the fear inseparable from living in a haunted world.

If we really look,
surely we can see
we are built for loving.
We are built open,
as capacity
for the other one.

January 16

The consciousness
in me and in you
is the One Consciousness
that creates all reality,
that is responsible for all reality.
I say:
Don't believe this.
Test it.

Here, search as I may,
I can find no decision making or maker,
no ideas or feelings or impressions of my own
—bright or dull—no mind at all
but only this bare Consciousness or Awakeness
that reads as absolutely clueless, useless,
incompetent, idiotic.
(No, I'm not playing modest, cross my heart.)
Yet what's needed is coming up
from the depths,
just when it should.
In Heaven
you discover this quiet upsurge
from the Abyss.
Try it out, learn to trust it,
and go on relying on it more and more.
Here is never-failing inspiration for non-persons.

January 18

You haven't a clue
or a resource you can claim,
and you get all the clues you can use.
It's like standing at the footlights of the world
smitten with amnesia,
but marvellously prompted
from the dark depths of the orchestra.

This Non-Being
is below Being, below Consciousness,
below everything,
so there's nothing Here to reveal,
nothing Here to come up with.
It's beyond and below everything.
So how do you know anything about it?
Well, you can see what it comes up with:
the yellow flowers, the universe.
And without the universe,
as the expression of this ineffable Origin,
there's no ineffable Origin.

The divine love of this Big One
is unconditional.
It makes no demands,
looks for no return,
is equally bestowed on all,
doesn't vary in the slightest,
always runs smooth.
Why?
Because the Big One lies at the Source of all,
and to be here
is to love all beings as Oneself,
regardless of how lovable or unlovable they may seem.

Just as I now *see* here,
in front of this page and this hand,
Nothing
(total absence of shape, structure,
limits, opacity, colour, movement),
so I now *hear*,
this side of the sounds
(birdsong, car-noises, children shouting)
that are coming and going in it,
Silence.
Equally I now *smell* here, thankfully,
no trace of tobacco smoke or cooking or drains.
Thus this First Person is illuminated by *every* sense,
as the unchanging and indispensable foreground
of all these ever-changing sensations.
In my exploration of *others*
I use what senses are available, as best I can;
in my exploration of *Myself*
I use them all
to perfection.
What is here to go wrong?

January 22

Seeing very often says,
wait!
It very often says,
don't know!
It looks feeble.
But it is in the nature of seeing to be inactive,
waiting for the answer,
not in a hurry.
It is a very positive thing to do,
to attend.
It is a kind of prayer:
praying for the answer to come clear.
Sometimes one has to wait a longish time,
and that is okay.

Encouraged by the great tradition
of the Inner Light
at my core,
and inspired
by my direct vision of it,
I submit with reverence
to what it lights up.
Here I am at once
this central Awareness or Consciousness
and what it's conscious of,
which is none other than
its own region-by-region embodiment,
its cosmic constitution.
The view out from here
embraces the One-centred
but many-levelled physique
that is the expression and instrument and object
of the Consciousness that I Am,
and I take it as I find it.

January 24

When I'm at my best,
when the most persistent and authentic
of my feelings are given full play,
I make a double discovery:
on the one hand I find myself shedding
all responsibilities,
all attachments and identifications whatever,
dropping the lot,
claiming nothing and being nothing,
and so at last breaking free;
and on the other hand (supremely inconsistent)
I find myself
taking everyone and everything on board,
laying claim to the lot,
not resting content
until the universe's meanest creature
is gathered under my loving wing.
This is the ultimate truth,
the paradoxical and double-sided truth
about the way I really feel.

Seeing who I am is
a strangely physical experience.
It is like an energy, an empowering,
a physical tone, an uplift,
a rootedness, courage,
a faring forth into the world.
It is enlivening.

Even in ordinary life
we find hints of this vital connection
between Self-awareness and creativity.
Don't our very best moments always include
a heightened consciousness of ourselves,
so that we aren't really lost in inspiration
or creative fervour or love,
but newly found?
At its finest,
doesn't the opaque object over there
point unmistakably back
to the transparent Subject here?
It may even happen that the transparency comes first:
we attend,
our idiotic chatter dies down,
we consciously become nothing
but this alert, expectant Void:
and presently the required tune or picture,
the key notion, the true answer,
arises ready-made in that Void,
from that Void.

So thoroughly have we insulated
the human from the cosmic
that when at last they are brought together
the effect may well prove overwhelming,
as the pent-up energy is discharged
in a flash of illumination
revealing
undreamed-of beauty.

Enlightenment is total open-mindedness,
transparency, simplicity,
taking nothing for granted.
In one word, it is
discovery.
What is to be discovered is
your own nature.
Who are you?
Only you
are in a position to find out,
because everyone else
is elsewhere, off-centre.
Only you
can investigate what it is to be you.

There's no such thing as a true enlightenment
which doesn't light up every creature
on Earth and in the skies,
however grotesque or remote or unlovable.
How could we begin to disentangle ourselves
from any part of
the One
in whom we live and move
and have our being?
Enlightenment is cosmic
or an illusion.

It is always the *other* that I fear,
hate, envy, plan to destroy.
Prove to me that there's a level
on which I *am* you,
and you *are* me,
and all aspects
of our mutual alienation
are ended.

Here,
I'm enjoying that face of yours
as mine.
Here,
I *have* you as object
and *am* you as subject,
and so take on both your appearance
and your reality.
What could be more intimate than
this double intimacy?
How could I fear you
who are myself?

February 1

No wonder the essential Experience
is dismissed so cavalierly,
is so unwelcome and so distrusted.
Below the surface we are all terrified
of our Emptiness.
Till it's inexhaustible and breathtaking
beneficence and fertility
begin to take shape, it must seem
(to many of us if not to all)
not just meaningless but suicidal,
mere annihilation.

When people say they don't see it
they generally mean they don't *feel* it:
the inner landscape leaves them cold.
But of course it does!
Thank God for that.
This is a matter of fact and not of feeling,
of one's eternal and natureless Nature
and not of the ever-changing kaleidoscope
of thoughts and emotions
it gives rise to.
It's the truth that sets us free
—the Truth that couldn't be more plain—
plain in the sense of cool and undecorated,
and plain in the sense of unhidden.

February 3

The only way to do something about
our feelings, perhaps not very much,
is to go upstream of feelings
and see Who has them.
So feelings,
whether negative or positive,
are an opportunity
for seeing
Who we are.

It's not symmetry; it's asymmetry.
It's feelings to no-feelings.
The space I am is not a feeling space.
It's capacity for feeling.
My nature always
is
to be free
from what is filling it.

When you see who you really are,
you will not find that
your feelings are all positive.
Well, I don't find that.
Feelings are up and down.
Douglas is anxious, then he's not anxious,
then he's happy, then he's less happy.
He's continually changing.
That makes life interesting.
But who I am
here
is not subject to those variations.

Who I really am
is
my blessing,
my refuge.

February 7

The initial seeing
gives the ability to renew it.
Since the Absence of things here
is as plainly visible and as cooly factual
as their presence there,
the seeing of this Absence
is available immediately, anytime,
at will.
Unlike ideas and feelings,
you can have this simple seeing
when you need it most,
as when you are agitated or worried.
It's ready to hand
for dealing with troubles
as they arise,
on the spot.

This meditation is certainly not in itself
a mystical or religious experience,
not euphoric,
not a sudden expansion
into universal love or cosmic consciousness,
not any kind of feeling or thought
or intuition whatever.
Quite the contrary,
it is absolutely featureless, colourless, neutral.
It is gazing into
the pure, still, cool, transparent
Fountainhead,
and simultaneously out from It
at the streaming, turbulent world,
without being carried away into that world.

You can ensure your full share of
mystical or spiritual experiences,
not by going downstream after them,
but only by noticing that you are
forever
upstream of them all,
and they can only be enjoyed there
from their Source in you.

Seeing who one is,
the simple vision
here,
is the root.
It is without quality.
It has nothing to recommend it.
It's naked,
absolutely naked,
and that is why it is so valuable,
why it is available whatever one's mood.
One doesn't have to psych oneself up.

February 11

First see who you are
now.
Then you will surely find that
only the truth sets you free,
and all of it is clearly presented
at this moment,
if you stop thinking about it
and look,
and take seriously what you see.

When overlooked and avoided,
this Absence
reads as useless and boring,
the shadow of a shadow,
a dead loss.
Or worse: as more terrifying than
any ghost or devil.
When taken in and taken on, however,
it becomes
the Presence
that is my treasure.

FEBRUARY 13

This despised No-thing at my back
turns out to be far more real
than any of the things in front of me.
This neglected Place
is a truer one
than any on the map,
for, in contrast to them,
it's infinitely wide and deep,
uniformly itself through and through,
all on show at once,
always accessible,
unchanging and
– ah! –
my Native Land,
the Big Country:
the Country of Everlasting Clearness.

FEBRUARY 14

Seeing what you really are is just about the easiest thing in the world to do, and just about the most difficult to keep doing: at first. Normally, it takes months and years and decades of coming back home, to the spot one occupies (or rather, doesn't occupy: the world does that) before one learns the knack of remaining centred, of staying indoors, of living from one's space instead of from one's face. Nevertheless, now you know how to get there, you can visit home whenever you wish and whatever your mood. And, once over the threshold, you're perfectly at home: here, you can't put a foot wrong. Practice doesn't *make* perfect here: it *is* perfect from the start. You can't half see your facelessness now, or see half of it. There are no degrees of enlightenment: it is all, or nothing.

FEBRUARY 15

Don't believe
but test
what I'm saying to you:
that all things,
never mind what,
when consciously observed
from their Origin,
are bathed in its perfume
and lit up
with its radiance.

There is a glory.
Always.
To find it,
be
Where
it comes from.

How much harder it is
to bear
one's splendour
than
one's miseries!

We discover
at our heart
the power and the glory
behind the world.
This is the message of
all the great religions:
at your heart is the kingdom
and the power and the glory.
Not because you deserve it.
It's grace.
Far from deserving it,
on the contrary,
it's a free gift,
begging to be noticed.

Meister Eckhart said:
"My dear friend,
what have you got to lose
by doing God the favour of
letting God be God in you?"
Think of that!
This is the message
of all the great mystics of whatever religion,
although not couched in
such beautiful language.
It is awesome and it's astounding:
the Treasure
which is so neglected
at our hearts.

FEBRUARY 19

If I am perfectly contented now,
it is because I have ceased to be
any kind of Container at all,
but instead am con*tent* with my *con*tent.

When I am consciously at large,
no longer a thing among things,
a consciousness
among consciousnesses,
I am Liberated,
and the world,
in spite of everything,
is all right
because it is all me.

In plain language,
my psychological problems
all boil down to the problem of
my Identity.
They are settled only
by attending to the One here,
to this First Person
who is supposed to have them.
Here
is the only profound analysis,
the only therapy
which penetrates to the Root of the trouble,
the only lasting cure of my disease.

Though the results
may be slow to manifest
(and then be more manifest
to others than to me),
this way is economical,
thorough, foolproof,
well-tested over thousands of years,
instantly available, and
(though in a sense it costs the Earth)
quite *gratis*.
Freedom is free.

This immense and self-aware
emptiness
that I find here
isn't just empty.
It's empty-for-filling.
Ultimately no-one and nothing
is left out.
In fact I'm not well,
not quite sane,
not 'all there',
not whole
till I'm
the Whole.

There are no fates, factors or forces
outside the First Person that I am,
working against me.
Even the 'nastiest' things that
happen to me as third person are
in reality
my profound intention
as First Person.
So I say Yes! to life,
and this is the true therapy.

This Abyss below the Line,
this Beyond
which is beyond Heaven and Hell
and existence itself,
but nevertheless absolutely real,
is all-important for us because
it happens to be
our refuge,
our healing.

Only God,
our Whole,
is the completion,
the healing remedy
of the fragments that we are.
He is what we want,
and we are not ourselves
without Him.
We are lost
till
we are lost
in Him.

When I see
this true and ultimate identity,
I see it for and as
the One we all are,
the One who *is*.
Our enlightenment
cannot help but spill out
on all beings,
for the simple reason that
we are them.

Our meditation cures bashfulness,
not by enabling you
to lose yourself
in the objective world,
but by enabling you
to find yourself,
as its Container.

FEBRUARY 29

Tell me, what's impossible
for the One that creates Itself?
And what's impossible
for those who enjoy
union with that One?

We are all
more or less ill
till we find
by Self-enquiry
our Oneness
with
everyone else.

March 2

When you see the truth,
you are doing it for others
as much as for yourself,
because Who is doing it
is not an individual.
Who is doing it
is the One
who is the inside story of
all these contestants
on the face of the Earth.

We all have different functions.
Some of us are active behind the scenes
helping the world secretly
by something like prayer or awareness,
because awareness is not separate from the world.
The best that you can do for suffering beings
is see Who you and they really are.
Underground this will affect everybody profoundly,
because you are doing it *as* them and *for* them.

March 4

When I identify
with the guy in the mirror,
he turns his back on the world.
He says, "I've got enough troubles of my own.
Keep out."
The One you really are
never can turn her back on the world.
She embraces the world.
She is the world.
This is not because you are special.
You always were this way.

MARCH 5

The sublimely remote
transcendent Deity
can mean nothing to man
if it finds no lodgement
in his inmost heart;
and the Deity
that is thus born in him
is no Deity
if it is his own,
and is not referred to a wholly external source.

March 6

I very much believe that,
if there is to be a next big step
in our evolution,
it will be this step to the Centre:
the step from our present kind of consciousness
will be to the new kind of First Person,
concentric consciousness.
Utopia would be in no danger of breaking out,
but just imagine the Renaissance!

MARCH 7

Here
we sink our differences;
or rather,
we sink
and leave our differences
floating.
All action is stooping to conquer,
where stooping is
absolute abasement.

MARCH 8

The Whole lacks nothing.
But even the Godhead needs
a photosphere to shine,
feathers to fly,
legs to walk our earth,
fins to swim.
Every setting-board is a Calvary,
every collector's pin a crucifier's nail.
Every dust-grain,
every electron and proton,
every point-instant,
is Bethlehem;
every nest the manger-cradle;
every womb Mary's.

God is indivisible.
This is so marvellous because it means
the whole of God
is
where you are:
not your little bit of God,
but the whole of God.
If we resist this,
it's because we are resisting
our splendour, our greatness.

MARCH 10

When we reach Him
there is only Himself,
and His proof is our disproof.
It is only by complete loss
of individuality,
by reduction to nothing,
that the great saint can become
the vehicle of the Whole
which is the perfect individual.

I don't say that what is done consciously
from my Centre,
by Who I really am,
by What I really am,
is perfect
(because it's out in the world
and therefore imperfect)
but it's done incredibly better
than my little self could do it.

MARCH 12

The whole practical business of life
is shifting trust
from what you look like
to what you are,
from what you have been advertised to be
to what you really, really are.
In other words:
surrender
to the will of God.

The know-how of our Centre
is fabulous.
If you want to do anything well,
I don't care what it is,
(as long as it is half way legal,
perhaps I should add!)
do it from the Source.
If you want to do it badly
you do it from the periphery.

MARCH 14

Fortunately what matters,
what gives relief
from our stress and distress,
isn't our *knowledge* of
the Great Beyond
(it is absolutely unknowable,
most of all to itself)
but our *direct perception* of it.

Only This can be clearly seen
because only This is so simple,
so clear and plain
and all-on-show
that it just cannot be mis-seen.
Only This can be perfectly got
because only in This
is there nothing to get.
Only This
can insure against and repair
the ravages of time because
only This is timeless.

March 16

Here
you come to recognise
and increasingly give way to
the practical flair,
the astounding know-how,
of the very Source of things.
More and more
Who you are
is allowed to look after
what you are,
unhindered.

Only This
can be safely relied upon because
only This
neither relies upon
nor needs any foundation whatever:
it has the useful knack of
hoisting itself out of the Inane,
out of the Dead Blank,
by its own boot-straps.
If you can't trust the One
who has this impossible know-how,
who or what can you trust?

March 18

There's no occasion in our working or leisure life
when it's inappropriate or inefficient
to live from the truth.
Agreed that the truth, so easy to see,
is so hard to keep on seeing.
But is life without it less hard?
Is life lived from a many-sided lie
a practical proposition?
Let's remember, let's take courage from the fact
that our practice isn't changing our lifestyle,
but noticing how we're living in any case:
as this Empty fullness,
as this truly amazing union of
perfect freedom and total involvement.

Attend,
as if for the first time,
to the one Spot in the world that
only you are in a position to inspect,
to the Point
that only you have inside information about,
and witness
its immediate explosion to
world-wide dimensions.

Do what you like to me,
I will live
from what I see is here,
not from what you say is here.
And I will tell the world about it.
And I will take the consequences.
Meanwhile, I swear to you that
to live from this is really to live.
Which is to live Godly.

The whole aim of my work
is practical:
it is how to live from
what I can see is the case,
what is true,
rather than from social fiction,
concepts, wishy-washy stuff.

MARCH 22

Whatever I'm doing
from the delusion and nonsense that
there is a thing here doing it,
is worse done,
and whatever I'm doing
from my Space
is better done.

The primary and saving whole truth
is that we are all living from
our Space
and not our face.
We are all doing it right.
We are all firmly and forever
established
in our True Nature.
To be at all is to be
Being.

March 24

The big thing for me, a development over the last few years, is the realization of the Incarnation. To put it simply: if it is true what Tennyson says, what the Koran says, that God is nearer to me than my hands and my feet and my breathing, then God is Here and This is where he lives. This is the temple of the living God, and these hands are not coming out of an organism Here: I see that they're coming out of the Space. Then these hands do a different job, these feet go on the errands of God, and this voice speaks his words. They are the instruments of Who we really are. This is a very different organism from the one we see in the mirror and see around us. This is the First Person, and the First Person is totally different from the third person.

MARCH 25

The great reminder
is when you've got someone in front of you.
Shall you lie
and say it's confrontation,
or shall you tell the truth
and see it's face to Space?
Then love can flourish.
I am not saying that
this guarantees
love
but that telling the truth
gives love a much better chance.

March 26

Till the loss of one's head
issues in the finding of one's
heart
—a heart so tender
that it is mortally wounded
by the world's appalling suffering—
till then one
falls
far short of the goal which is
the love
that transmutes all suffering.

We are built to die
for each other:
to disappear
in each other's favour.
We are built
for loving.

MARCH 28

What is
the heart and substance of love?
To put it at its most basic:
to love is to disappear
in someone's favour.
You vanish
in favour of that person.

The more I take care of
the Coolness
here
the more the warmth
takes care of itself
there.
It's not that I feel myself to be
more loving
(my love goes out to you
and cannot be retained here)
but that you are seen
to be
more lovable.

March 30

For it's not as if,
arriving at this No-man's-land
and No-things'-land,
(or, if you like, at this Never-never-land)
one comes to a *dead* end,
to a region so nonexistent
that it could hold no meaning
and excite no interest.
Exactly the reverse.
It is that Unknowable
from whose depths the known gushes
without reason and without stint,
that Unthinkable Seed
of all life and all thought:
including *this* thought about It.
It is that Face
that is masked by every face.

Seeing is not concerned with feeling,
it is concerned with fact.
When I see Who I am
I find that my very nature is
openness.
In a certain non-sentimental, non-feeling sense,
Seeing is loving
because Seeing is totally dying for the other
and really being annihilated for the other.
It is not in the realm of feeling or thinking.
It is more fundamental.
It does not feel
as one would expect love to feel,
but I think it is, shall I say,
a specially deep kind of loving.
So deep that the feeling is left floating.
It goes beneath the feeling to the fact.
It is not a kind of embryo loving or inferior loving,
it is a culmination of loving.

I find I've never been
face to face
with anybody.
This permanent asymmetry
is the beginning of
love
and the end of fear.
Imagining I've any shield or wall
here
to keep you out with
is rejection of you,
separation from and fear
and even hatred of you.
The remedy
is to see
that I'm built open:
built for loving.

All true lovers are,
however unconsciously,
face to no-face.
Conversely,
all the consciously faceless are,
at least in the profoundest sense,
true lovers.
This is how our love-life is lived
when we stop pretending.
Really we are built this way
and have no choice.

April 3

Can any lover
know what love is
who prudishly refuses entry to
the loved one's face
(as if it were possible!)
by always thrusting his or her own
in the way?
Can any lover
fail to know what love is
who submits to this invasion
so delightedly,
when to look at
is to die for
the loved one?

My only claim to this hand
is that when it is hurt I am hurt,
and what it touches I touch,
and all its deeds are mine;
and my only claim to Humanity
is that I am responsible for my neighbour,
wherever he lives
and whatever he does.
For until I am him
I am not myself.
To know myself
I must study him,
and to be at peace with myself
I must love him:
all my hatred is self-hatred.

April 5

Observe
what a perfect set-up it is:
that while the *sight* of
Who you really are
is forever the same and complete,
the *meaning* of what you see
is inexhaustible,
capable of endless enrichment.
Observe
how you need both, together,
and how naturally they converge
and become inseparable,
given a little time and attention.

Whereas
the Experience of our Nature
is served up (if at all) complete,
in one infinitely generous helping,
its Meaning
is for the most part withheld.
Normally it's doled out in driblets,
at other times poured out
more generously,
but never given in its entirety.
The last word about
This
is never said,
the ultimate and all-embracing idea of It
is never conceived,
the deepest feeling never plumbed.

APRIL 7

It is the mark of our life
at its best
when we place it
in its full hierarchical setting,
so that it becomes
an utterly different thing,
a sacrament,
universal,
profound.

What is the purpose of life?
As I see it, and as the great mystics
of all the great religions saw it,
the purpose of life is a simple one:
it is conscious union with our Source.
Our Source offers the incredible privilege of
union with Him or Her or It.
As Meister Eckhart said,
"God's in, I'm out."
He puts it very beautifully:
"Put on your jumping shoes and jump into God."
It's jumping from your appearance to your Reality.
I love that.
It is our business
to jump
into the place we never left.

APRIL 9

Look *down* at yourself,
at your own Bottom Line or Ground,
and you'll see with unmatched clarity
the Place
where what you look like
flips over
into What you really, really are;
and where You
as Root
start to quicken and burgeon
and blossom and bear fruit
as the world itself,
eternally.

This wide-open-mouthed Appetite
for the world
is what I Am
right here and now,
and It is infinitely mysterious.
Truly I can't say *what* It is
but only *that* It is.
Here is not a case of
I am this or that or the other,
but plain
I Am.
And, back of the I Am,
the I Am Not
from which it arises,
without reason and without stint.
A case of Being,
without being someone or something.

APRIL 11

The thrilling bottom line is that I
(I don't mean myself as a person, I mean the real I)
is absolutely hidden
from Itself.
I know myself as
unknowable.
I'm rooted and grounded in
complete mystery,
unknowability,
ineffablity,
unawareness.

God's own knowledge of Himself
is that He can't understand Himself,
can't make head or tail of Himself.
God has no clue to how
he invented Himself.
God doesn't really know
how He did it!
He is bowled over,
absolutely
and
forever.

APRIL 13

To go forward in life
not knowing who you are
or where you're coming from is
poetry.
These people who use expressions like
'the dark desert of the Godhead
where God is unknown to Himself'
speak to my heart very much.
One casts oneself
into that wild sea.
What I can understand,
what I can know,
what I can get taped,
will not satisfy
my heart
or my mind.

Basically, the trouble with my mind
is the conviction I've got one;
and returning it to store
—to the Universe at large
or, in Zen terms, to
'Great Space'
or the
'One Mind'—
is enough to set it in order.

April 15

While I'm seeing what I really am
as First Person
I'm clear-headed and clear-minded
and clear of body and mind at all levels,
with their attendant problems.
And while I'm not seeing this
I have plenty of problems,
all of which are reducible to the problem
of this morbid growth called brain/head/mind,
this malignancy flourishing
right here
at the mid-point of my universe.
To say that this wen-like cancer gets in my way
and blocks my light is an understatement.
It maddens me,
and not less so for being quite imaginary.
This isn't so much *having* mental trouble
as gratuitously *making* trouble for myself,
at the one Spot which needs to be trouble-free,
and manifestly is trouble-free, whenever I attend to it.
Enlightenment, which is shining the light steadily
on this obstructionless Spot,
isn't something I can manage without.

It really is so very inefficient
to operate from a mind
which is full of things to go wrong,
and so very efficient
to operate from a
No-mind
which is empty
of all that chatter.
This isn't a dogma for believing
but a working hypothesis
for testing,
all day and every day.

APRIL 17

One's mind awakens.
Ideas, inspiration,
guidance from moment to moment,
flow without obstruction
from their Source,
which is experienced here
as Itself
mindless.
Paradoxically,
to be really creative,
to be really intelligent about things
there,
one must be
a conscious numb-skull
here,
empty-headed,
clueless,
blank.

The trouble with the mind
is its supposed abstraction
from the world,
its supposed condensation
into a nuclear thing
here.
The mind goes wrong
by misapprehending
where it is
and to whom it belongs.

I am truly broad-minded
to the degree that my mind,
let go of,
alights on and merges with and irradiates
the whole scene.
There it comes into its own.
To be opinionated, narrow-minded,
under pressure, depressed, repressed:
all such diseases of the mind
arise from its displacement and resulting compression.
Given back to the world,
returned to where it came from,
it expands and recovers.
At large again, it is infinitely large and generous.

All the complexes and problems
of the mind
arise from its overcrowding and congestion.
The cure isn't to reform it but just to
let it go
where it wants to go.
We are now letting it go
to where it belongs.
A tremendous relief!
This is not perfecting the mind
because the mind is imperfect in every way:
still one experiences sadness and confusion,
anxiety and pain, as well as positive feelings,
but they are seen as characterising the world
and not as personal hang-ups.
This relocation helps a lot
but is no recipe for continuous happiness,
or any kind of perfection
where happiness and perfection don't belong.
Only at Centre are you
All Right!

April 21

My mind,
with all its thoughts and feelings,
is centrifugal.
Ceasing to be a small, local, private,
personal possession abstracted from
the universe there and shut up
in a brain-box here (as if it could be!)
my mind is at large,
one with the universe,
blown sky-high.
The world, so seen, is the same old world,
yet utterly different.
It is replete with a mind and meaning
I no longer abstract from it.
It is all there,
because I claim none of it for myself.
It is sane.
It makes sense.
It is loved.

Only give it half a chance
and I guarantee
that you will find that this
No-thing
is the only thing
you never get sick to the back teeth of,
that never loses its charm,
that is always brand new,
that you
never, never
get used to.

April 23

One of the paradoxes of the
Emptiness here
is how,
though forever the same,
it gets more intriguing,
more surprising,
more wonderful,
more precious,
the more it is noticed.
Here,
and here
alone,
familiarity breeds
respect,
dedication,
reverence.

Then I remembered
that the great secret of life,
the great know-how,
is *not* to know,
to be at a loss.
To be,
precisely,
at my wit's end,
which is the beginning
of the Wit of the One
I really, really am.
How can the One
take over
so long as I'm determined
to hang on to little me?

APRIL 25

Every 'choice' that is made
from *not* knowing,
from *not* having it all taped,
from *not* having it in a briefcase,
from *not* having a script or a rule,
but from the
Clarity
here
and what fills it,
seems to me to be
a whole different deal,
the true
surrender.

A problem arises:
just come Home
and see what you get up to,
what you say,
what your hands do,
where your feet go.
If you are really going
Home
and acting from
Home,
what you do will be appropriate
for that occasion.

April 27

I find that, when I am seeing clearly Who's seeing, it is unnecessary—it is fatal to that seeing—to worry about what to say or do, to think or feel: the fitting expression of First Personhood occurs as a matter of course, spontaneously, according to circumstances. The outcome is unpredictable. If it proves unconventional, crazy, shocking, or even wicked by local third person standards, this can't be helped. In the long run, it is what's needed. I know how to wait, but cease dithering. When they are really required, the right things are done. So I don't resolve in advance not to be unloving and mean and petty and irritable, not to boast, over-eat, steal, flatter, despise, fret, sulk (the list is endless), though it may well turn out that such behaviour doesn't occur when I'm attentive to the Source of all behaviour. If I'm observed to be living up to any 'principles', this is an incidental and external view, for the One here is innocent of principles— and everything else.

At last, having learned the lesson
of countless disappointments,
and having ceased to rely on
the minuscule resources of that pinhead
over there in my mirror,
I start relying
on the infinite resources of the
Godhead,
on the Source of all resources
right here,
so that now I find myself
knowing what has to be known,
and saying what has to be said,
and doing what has to be done,
without any preview at all.
I don't know what I think
till I hear what I say:
hear the words that come from my
No-mouth:
from something like
what the Ancient Greeks would have called
my Daimon, or Good Genius.

April 29

I notice that I annihilate and re-create the world, while *people* merely close and open their eyes. I hush the world; they stop their ears. I spin the world; they pirouette. I transmute the world, turning legs into grass, into trees, into hills, into sky; *people* bend down and straighten up. I go up to the stars and toss the constellations around; *people* turn their faces to the night-sky. The toy chair, the wedge-shaped road, the dolls' houses, the mole-hole road tunnels—all swell to accommodate me, and shrink to nothing when I have no further use for them; *people* are obliged to shrink and swell to fit their surroundings. At will, I can see through a spoon, invert a cup without spilling the tea, squash a plate without touching or breaking it, get clean through a keyhole, transpose mountains, turn a house round. I can confer upon anyone or anything the supreme honour of being the focal point, the end-product and meaning, of the universe—and demote him or it again, instantly. Such are the powers of the First Person singular, the royal prerogatives of the shy King—the King who doesn't wish to know he is a king. His kingdom, the First Person universe, surpasses everything he had imagined.

The great thing is
to be
as simple as
God.
See what is given.
This is the marvellous thing.
If we would relax into
what is blazingly obvious,
we should find all that we need.
It is a kind, kind old world.
It hides nothing essential.
The more essential a thing is,
the more given it is.
We imagine it's the other way round.
What is really important
is given free
now.

MAY 1

I remember many years ago walking in the woods near my home in a state of great desperation because I kept on forgetting Who I was from time to time. I frequently found myself slipping back into third-personhood. The shades of the prison house would keep descending on me. How could I keep the Vision alive? It was a desperate state. In the end, I decided that I couldn't keep the Vision going at full strength. I just gave up. I said, "I can't do it." Then when I gave up, it was all right. I didn't have to keep the Seeing at high tension all the time. It's there in the background whatever happens. It really is, even when I am filling in my tax returns.

Yes,
you've got it!
You see
with total clarity
Who and What
you've always been,
namely this
Disappearance
in favour of others,
this Emptiness
which is aware of itself as
no-thing
and therefore all things.
How could we not see
this most obvious of all sights,
once our attention is drawn to it?

Congratulations!
You're enlightened!
You always were.

May 3

If I fail to see what I am
(and especially what I am not)
it's because I'm too busily imaginative,
too 'spiritual', too adult and knowing, too credulous,
too intimidated by society and language,
too frightened of the obvious
to accept the situation exactly as I find it
at this moment.
Only I am in a position to report on what's
here.
A kind of alert naivety is what I need.
It takes an innocent eye
and an empty head
(not to mention a stout heart)
to admit their own perfect emptiness.

The Experience of your Nature
is always transparent and complete.
In fact, till you see What you are
you don't know what obviousness is!
Only you
(the real You, you as you are for you, intrinsically)
are absolutely visible.
All else is more or less veiled.
Compared with this Sight
all other sights are obscure, fuzzy, groping, dim.
There's something unique about its obviousness,
a sharpness, a surprise,
a quiet thrill or *frisson*
that there's no proper word for.

MAY 5

I am at large
in the world.
I can discover no watcher here,
and over there something watched,
no peep-hole out into the world,
no window-pane,
no frontier.
I do not detect a universe:
it lies wide open to me.

Your true Nature
is the Paradox
to take care of all paradoxes:
there is nothing that is not you
and nothing that is you;
the Aware Space
is and isn't its contents;
you care
and you don't care;
you control things
and they just happen.
This may sound silly,
but in fact
it is the perfection of wisdom.
Also it works.

May 7

The spiritual life
is all paradox:
it's the union of opposites.
It's having your cherry cake
and eating it.
It finds you
on the way Home,
and all the way Home,
seated, with your feet up,
by the fire of God's love.

This peace
is our very nature,
not something we come across.
It's where we are,
nearer than all else.
We don't come *to* it,
we come *from* it.
To find it
is to allow ourselves
to go back
to the place we never left.

MAY 9

At the Centre is always perfection,
off-Centre always imperfection.
Human beings are (to say the least) lacking,
and no amount of seeing Who we really are
will make a human into an angel
or the human scene into Utopia, let alone Heaven.
The effects of our seeing will, if we persist,
certainly become evident
in our personality and environment,
but they will vary immensely
and will often seem to us
to be very meagre indeed.
One thing alone can be relied on
through all circumstances,
and that is our
Core of Peace.
Seers may often find themselves in a tragic
and sad and puzzling and troublesome world,
but we never (so long as we are seeing)
lack peace of mind.
Our basic anxiety has gone.
Seeing that we are indeed
Peace Itself,
we are at rest.

MAY 10

On the road,
waking at last
to the glaringly obvious fact
that it's the countryside
and never me
that's behaving frantically,
I'm apt to find myself
enjoying
a new and pleasurable
tranquility.

May 11

The Perennial Philosophy
has consistently and persistently
put forward a hypothesis
so amazing
and so delectable
(one's essential Godhood, no less!)
that it cries out to be tested
by every available means,
just in case
it should turn out
to be true.

MAY 12

At the very core of the great religious traditions (overlaid,
neglected, very often vehemently denied by religious experts,
but nevertheless the taproot those traditions spring from
and are sustained by) is one perfectly lucid, simple, awesome,
beautiful realisation. It's a proclamation which deserves all the
trumpets and bells of Heaven and Earth, and it's about you
personally. Personally. It is this: more intimately yours than all
else, "closer than breathing, and nearer than hands and feet"
(as Tennyson put it so accurately) is the One you really, really
are, the Self of yourself, the Self and Source and Substance of
all selves, the Alone. No mere spark are you of that Eternal
Fire, no mere ray of the One Light that lights every man and
woman and child that the world comes into. Not a part of
the Whole which (to quote Dante) "gathers up the scattered
leaves of all the universe and binds them by love into one
volume", but that Volume itself. You are all of that All which
is strictly indivisible. Repeat: indivisible.

May 13

The wonderful proposition
of all the mystics that I know,
and would care to call real mystics,
is that the heart of you,
the reality of your life,
the reality of your being,
your real self
is
the whole of God.
Not a little bit of that fire
but the whole fire.

The kingdom,
the power and the glory
is
at your very centre.
That's what you are looking out of,
where you are coming from:
Being itself, the Mystery.

MAY 15

The basic doctrine
of the Perennial Philosophy
is that you and I are
God herself
travelling incognito.
The one we all really are is
the one reality
behind all things,
call it God, Buddha-nature,
Atman-Brahman, or what you like.
What one is doing is only to connect up with
and celebrate and live from
this perennial wisdom,
which is to be found
at the very heart
of all the great religions.
There it is:
unrecognised, neglected, scorned, denied,
but there it is.
One is simply continuing in this tradition
as best one can.

As Divinity itself,
as the Space for all
and the Source of all,
you are responsible for all.
There is no second Power.
Who you really, really are
did it all,
is doing it all.

MAY 17

Notice
whether this Space that you are
is *efforting* its contents.
Do you, who are attending to the scene,
have any sense of intending it,
of contriving it
and cobbling it together,
of causing and maintaining it?
It is for you who are responsible for it to say.
Isn't it rather that
everything flows spontaneously,
without motive
or taking thought,
from your
Being:
a ceaseless spin-off from
Who you are?

Let's take a look at power: at who has it, and how much.
Now a man who is a little thing has a little power, or so at
any rate he believes. But a God who is No-thing has no
power at all, and a God who is All-things has all power. And
the Seer, the one who has seen off his humanhood and seen
in his Godhood, takes on with it this seeming paradox, this
same union of opposites. He is all-powerless and all-powerful,
willing nothing and willing everything. What this means in
his everyday life is that he so concurs in all God's arrangements
for him that he intends them. His will merges with God's, and
all happens as he wants it to happen. Not as he superficially
desires, of course, but as he deeply desires, in his heart. His
real joy and his *real* peace are to do the will of the One he
really is.

MAY 19

The only way
to unleash irresistible magic,
and to think and feel
without any negativity,
is consciously to station oneself
where one has always been anyway,
namely at the source of it all,
at the unthinkable
Origin
which is the only real Magician
and the only real Power
and the only real Affirmation
free from any trace of denial.
Rejoin that sole
and only positive Source,
and see
what your life is like.

That little one,
always seeking power over others,
turns out to be powerless.
By contrast,
this Big One,
altogether non-interfering,
turns out to be
the Only Power,
not operating from outside
on creatures
but from inside
as them.
This is not acting
from a position of weakness:
to be Space for the other
is a position of
enormous strength.
The Incomparable Safety!

May 21

Naturally you are all-powerful. You aren't all-powerful in the sense that you could, if you really pulled yourself together and got around to it, set up a model universe in which there's love without indifference and hate, courage without danger and fear, goodness without evil, beauty without dreariness and ugliness, life without death. No: you can no more make these improvements than you can make black whitewash or silent bangs. The list of the things that even you can't do is endless. All the same, you are all-powerful in the sense that, accepting the coexistence and clash of opposites as the price (a terribly high price, but not prohibitive) of a cosmos, you let out an almighty Yes! to it all: Yes! throughout it all and in spite of it all; Yes! because this (in all its astounding and awful and lovely detail) is what you *are*; and Yes! because you *will* what you are.

We put limits on God
because we don't realize what He has already done,
what His mere Being entails.
His mere Being entails the impossible,
and after that
everything is comparatively straightforward and easy,
if I may speak that way.
It puts in perspective our headaches and concerns.
It really puts them in perspective.
It helps one,
(I am talking about a rather low, practical level now)
it really helps one to put up with things as they are, alas,
when one sees where they come from.

Hooray!

May 23

While it remains true
that this instant seeing into my Timeless Nature
is effortless and free,
it's also true that *it works out in my life
only to the extent that it's worked at.*
The discovery
that I am absolutely all right as I am
– as I Am –
has to be actualised
by its patient rediscovery,
and rediscovery, and rediscovery,
till all traces of artifice and effort,
all sense of attainment,
have vanished:
till it has become
in ordinary day-to-day living
what it always was in fact,
one's natural state.

To un-thing yourself
when all's going well
is good habit-forming practice.
But un-thinging yourself
when all's going badly
is better still.
Then the act of homing-in
makes a deeper impression,
and life in future
is that much less likely
to catch you out,
or napping.

MAY 25

It remains a stern fact that,
while it's the easiest thing imaginable
to see yourself intermittently as
bare Capacity,
it's far from easy to keep up the
seeing.
But isn't this contrast
what we deeply desire?
What is life without
audacity and daring,
without adventure,
without a tremendous challenge
to put us on our mettle?

What challenge
can compare with
this one great adventure
which is never completed,
yet is ever complete,
because you can enjoy
being at the goal
from the very first step along the road?
Furthermore, this is not a big hard thing to do
made up of little hard things to do.
Each is as easy as winking.
Now.

May 27

It all began when, quite casually,
I happened to take a look
at the spot I occupy,
and found it unoccupied.
At once I saw how crazy I had been
to superimpose what I look like upon
what I am,
and then to lock onto that
fictional superimposition
for dear life.
How refreshing it was,
how good even for the body,
to relax one's stranglehold on it
and let it go
to where it belongs!

Seeing
was at first momentary.
It took many years and much practice
before it became habitual.
By practice I mean
renewal of the original experience
and not (repeat *not*)
adding anything to it.
By habitual I mean
remaining in contact with
one's central clarity
and not (repeat *not*)
clinging to it.

MAY 29

While time and practice
are needed, as a rule,
to establish Self-realisation,
they add nothing to the experience.
They habituate it, so that it's
no longer occasional or intermittent.
Also they allow it to take effect
in all the areas and levels
of one's life.

There is a great deal of difference between
seeing Who you are as a matter of some interest,
or help in time of need,
and a dedication to this as central in one's life.
But the commitment is not on the side of
or characteristic of the Centre itself.
The commitment is on the side of and (one hopes)
characterises the human periphery, the mind.
There is no commitment at the Centre.
The Centre is free of all characteristics.

May 31

This seeing is believing.
Altogether unmystical (in the popular sense),
it is a precise, total, all-or-nothing experience
admitting of no degrees.
Relief is instant and complete:
so long as it lasts.
But now the really exciting
part of the work begins:
you have to go on
seeing
your Absence/presence
whenever and wherever you can,
till the seeing becomes natural
and unbroken.

Seeing
is neither losing yourself in your
Emptiness
nor in what fills it,
but simultaneously viewing
the thing you are looking at and the
No-thing
you are looking out of.
There will be found no times when this
two-way attention
is out of place
or can safely be dispensed with.
The price of sanity is
vigilance.

June 2

What's the good of *talking about*
this world-transforming
shift of viewpoint
without *making* the shift,
and going on to stay shifted?
How to do just that?
By cultivating the habit of
seeing
that in fact it's no shift at all,
but simply
being
where you were all along,
at the world's Centre.

This meditation is eventually continuous.
There are no occasions
when it is inappropriate,
no times
when you may safely wander
from the First Person position.
In the end you stay at
Home
where it goes on
unbroken,
though at times unobtrusively,
as the bass accompaniment in music.

JUNE 4

If you really want to live
the aware life,
to wake up
from the social dream,
to be
Who you are,
everything
will spring to your aid
and push you towards
that supreme goal.

Attaining it
is realising you never left it.
Rather than *becoming* aware,
you experience Awareness as your very being.

I don't think we really value
our Source
until we discover
how desperately in need we are of
our Source
and
Centre
and
Resource.

JUNE 6

The true function of problems
is to direct you
to their solution
at the Centre.

At the centre
of my life
is
this Awareness
whose nature I find is
freedom:
freedom not only from thinghood
but from thoughts and feelings
of all kinds.
Certainly from problems of all kinds.
As the source of those things,
the origin of those difficult things,
it's business must be to leave them alone,
free
to be what they are.

June 8

Who I really am
doesn't in itself change
what I like to call my human nature.
What it does is
place it.
This difficult
and sometimes heart-rending stuff
is not denied.
In fact it is far more honestly reckoned with
and taken on board,
from the state of freedom
at the centre,
than ever it was from that illusory person.

Having some problems is very helpful.
Having quite severe problems
brings me back
to the place
where
there are no problems,
because Who I really am
is
problem free.
I'm living from
this problem-free area
out into the world.

June 10

The ups and downs of life,
(where you find life going on,
above that 'bottom line' of yours)
go on regardless of whether they are resented,
or just tolerated
or in the end
(whether by God's good grace,
or simple looking-to-see, or both)
welcomed with open arms.
The art of handling these inexorable goings-on
is the art of
resting
on what underlies them:
the art and science of
consciously
being
the ground
which supports all that commotion,
without itself becoming disturbed
in the slightest.
Here, you are the bedrock of the world,
where it all begins and where it all ends.
Eternally one and the same,
you are the Unmoved Mover.

The Source of all things
is concealed
at our very heart and centre.
The art of life
is to connect up
consciously
with this fantastic Resource.

JUNE 12

Think of all the energy we spend keeping up this fiction of a solid thing here. No animal and no infant has this handicap. Maintaining this lie of a central thing here is so wearing. Not only do we have to keep this block, this nut, in position (using up all that energy), but we have to keep on constantly adjusting it to deal with different people and different circumstances. Whereas, if I can leave them (those people out there), to take care of my thinghood, my appearance—of that lump if you wish—then I am relieved of all the expenditure of energy that that would involve. That's very practical. It makes lots of sense. And I promise you, it is really energising.

This Void
is
not
mere emptiness,
it is not mere
absence,
it is Self-Aware.
It is Self-Awareness
itself.
That makes it quite different
from a void which is
just an unconscious absence.

June 14

This Reality
has its own interior
self-justification.
It is
self-validating from
within
and when experienced
cannot be doubted.
It is
after all
what I'm most sure of,
because
I am
it.
All else is mere hearsay,
is off centre, remote, changing,
inscrutable, a product of ignorance.

This Clarity
I know
because I am it.
Here
I have inside information,
and only
here.
All the rest
is external acquaintance.

JUNE 16

One seeks in vain
for labels, worthy labels,
that will stick to this
Non-existence
which
is
infinitely
more real
than any of its products,
than anything which exists.

JUNE 17

Are we face to face,
in symmetrical relationship,
object confronting object,
each shutting out the other?
Quite the contrary.
Here where
I am
is no face,
no speck of anything
to ward you off with,
to resist your invasion.
Whether I like it or not,
I'm so wide open to you
that your face is mine
and I have no other.

June 18

I am
fully conscious
of the perfect way you give me
your face:
of the perfect way
I take it.
The way
I'm shaped and coloured
by that fascinating terrain
amazes and delights me.
Without fuss or comment or conditions
you supply my lack,
and I have no way of refusing.
I can only pretend to refuse you entry.

The practical difference this discovery makes
to your relationships
is
immense
and cumulative.
In fact what it comes to is that
you aren't *related* in any way to anyone:
you *are* that one.
Here,
undiscriminating love
is
your very Nature.

JUNE 20

If we really look
at what it's like where we are,
surely we can
see
we are built for
loving,
we are built
open,
we are built as
capacity
for the other one.
We disappear in favour of
the other,
not because we are very nice
or very loving people really,
but because this is the way we are.
We vanish in favour of
that one there.

If I am relating to my boss or my employee or my wife or my child, it is going to make an enormous difference if I experience myself as *Space for them to happen in*. It means that I am going to let them be what they are, because Space has no way of manipulating and using and exploiting them. Space is very patient, very hospitable. In a certain sense it is the very basis of loving. If one experiences oneself as Space for the other, one listens, one looks, one attends to the other. And the other one feels attended to, feels entertained and valued, because after all, if you have nothing where you are—no face, no thing at all— that other one is doing you the marvellous service of supplying you with this fascinating scene, this fascinating personality there, this warm human personality that is filling your Space.

If we tell it like it is, and are truthful about what we are for ourselves, we see that we are built open, built for loving. I do recommend this most highly as immensely practical— imperative I would say—for good personal relationships.

June 22

It is true, also, that the days or weeks or months following
your initial seeing (whether it came explosively or not) are
liable to prove joy-filled and light-some. You feel new-born
into a new world. But sooner rather than later, alas, all this
fades—much to your surprise and disappointment. "It does
nothing for me!" The temptation is then to give up the
meditation, under the mistaken impression that you have
lost the art of it. In fact, if you persist nevertheless, it comes
to be valued less for its appetising but incidental fruits than
for itself—for the plain and savourless truth of it, for the
nothing which it does indeed do for you, instead of the
something it used to do, and this is a great advance. Beginning
to lose interest in the fruits, you ensure they grow all the more
healthily, unobserved and undisturbed, and ripen in season.
Meantime, and always, your sole business is their nourishing
Root.

Our resistance to
seeing
Who we are
is largely due to the fact that
seeing we are nothing
seems to be the end of the story.
If we can quickly go on
to perceive that,
as nothing,
we are
also all things,
that it's a case of trading
one little guy for the whole world,
then we can see it's very good business.
It's not losing out.
Quite the contrary.

JUNE 24

I find in me two wills:
one that belongs to the pre-mortem life
of the one in my mirror,
and the other which belongs to the post-mortem life
of the one this side of my mirror.
The former is quick to say No!
to a good half of what happens to me,
while the latter eventually says
Yes!, So Be It!,
to it all.
And does so with good reason:
I see that right here all my resistance is dissolved
and I'm burst wide open to receive
whatever's in store for me.
Saying Yes! to it is often excruciatingly difficult, of course,
but it turns out to be the recipe
for the only peace worth having.
And so at last the paradox holds:
it's because I have no will that my will is done.
Right here,
total impotence and total omnipotence
come to the same thing.

You as the Whole of you
are responsible for everything,
and manage it all very well:
and this without any sense of responsibility
or good management.
How can you know this for sure?
Only by being yourself now
and consulting your firsthand experience.
Only by ceasing to masquerade
as a man, a woman, or a child.

The simple
but truly devastating fact
is
that
Who I really, really am
is
what you
and
all others
really, really are.

Consider what spiritual training would mean for the First person, for the one here. It would mean one is anxious to get something, whereas in fact one is complete. It would mean one is looking for future results, whereas in fact the Goal is Now or never. It would mean drawing comparisons with others' attainments, whereas in fact this one is incomparable. It would mean making enormous efforts to curb the wandering mind, whereas in fact it's trying so hard that's the trouble. It would mean sitting at the feet of some guru, or attempting to master the scriptures, whereas in fact it's this sort of indoctrination from outside which prevents discovery right here. It would mean dwelling on prescribed ideas (such as impermanence, no-self, non-duality) whereas in fact they would only cloud the Emptiness here: what's needed is to drop all ideas and stay perfectly open. It would mean cultivating feelings (such as compassion, love, calm) whereas in fact they would only obscure this central Dispassion. It would mean the hard grind of keeping up one's exercises, so many hours a day, day in and day out for years, in the teeth of all natural impulses, whereas in fact the divine ease I'm seeking so painfully is painlessly available here this very instant.

JUNE 28

If we practise the Beatific Vision in order to reap one day its advertised benefits, (peace, joy, freedom, creativity, and the rest) we aren't likely to garner a rich harvest. Whereas if we do so for its own sake and with no *arrière-pensée*, because living from the amazing Truth has got to be better right now and to make more sense than living from the socially-laid-down pack of lies, we are much more likely to gain all the unsolicited and unimaginable gifts that await us. In fact it is God Himself, not His bulging haversack of gifts, that is the real Gift, bestowed with infinite generosity.

The Absence
is
for acceptance as absence,
not as the presence of
a well-concealed gold-mine.
The gold comes out all right,
but unsought,
in its own good time
and
unpredictable
shape.

When you start living
the heroic life
(that is, living from your true Nature)
your peripheral and human nature
is bound to benefit.
You cannot know
in advance
how or when,
but you can count on
Yourself
the superhuman hero
giving yourself the human non-hero
a helping hand and a leg up
where necessary.

It would be difficult to overstate
the practical importance of this discovery,
its consequences for everyday living.
All alienation, all separation,
the many-sided threat
of hostile things and persons and situations:
these are no more than bad dreams.
All is You.
How could you fear Yourself?
How could you despise, resent, be bored by
Yourself?
How could you not love
Yourself?

Who or what am I
in my own experience?
Am I a thing
consumed with fear and anxiety
and soon to perish and be forgotten,
or am I
the No-thing
which includes things of different life-spans,
from galaxies to particles to people?

Things come and go
within
my Space,
which is not
the kind of thing that comes and goes.
Therefore I am not frightened.
I am not scared out of my wits
if I really live
from
Who I am and What I am,
which
is
my No-thingness,
which is
absolutely safe.

July 4

Incomparable Safety
is
at your Centre.
Incomparable
Safety!
Because No-thing
is
absoluteley safe.
The aware No-thing
where you are
is
not the kind of thing
that can be destroyed.

Yet it's no bad thing to be fearful,
provided we're driven to the one refuge
from all danger and stress and fear:
to this incomparable Safety,
to the Place or No-place
we have all along been at.
By pointing a finger,
or simply looking at What we're looking out of
at this moment,
or by any other means that works for us,
let's get Home to What we are.
Let's stay with and live from
this absolutely safe Reality
instead of that accident-prone appearance
in our mirror,
and see what comes of it,
what happens to our stress.

July 6

All this choosing one thing in preference to another is illusory, a great cover-up. Separate individuals, as such, are powerless to make the slightest difference in a universe where every one of them is tightly controlled by the rest. Pretending otherwise, (pretending that, as our sole selves, we exercise free will), is as absurd and dishonest as it is vainglorious—and stressful. Only the Source of all, under the sway of none, has free will; and only deeds which are seen to proceed from it, which are referred back to it, which are felt to be its own deeds—only these carry its marvellous smell, the smell of an originality and rightness which belongs solely to that Origin. To live the choiceless life that we have been describing is not fatalism. It is not giving up the struggle and accepting that one is a machine within a Machine. It is to identify with the Machine's Inventor, to take one's stand in Freedom itself. It is to be one's Source, to choose what flows from it, and to perceive it as very good.

So it all comes back to the crucial question
of my true Identity.
If I insist on making an object and a thing
and a third person of myself here,
I am consumed with a thousand fears
and better off dead.
But if I give up this unrealistic and unrewarding habit
and come to Myself,
I see that I have never emerged
from that marvellous Abyss,
that before Abraham was I am,
before the first galaxy and the first atom,
before time itself.
Right here and now,
in the very place all this stormy weather
of time and change
come from,
I am Home and dry.
Where can I go from this Safe Haven?

JULY 8

What a relief
to be
backed by the One
whose name
is
I Am,
the name that precedes and introduces
every other name!
What a relief
to merge into
and
be
upheld by
the Unlimited.

I promise you that the rewards will be proportional to the seriousness and persistence of your Homecoming. But they will be unique to you, and I can't predict them in any detail. There are four things, however, that I can safely say:

1. The more you go for the real truth and the less for the rewards, the more rewards you will get.

2. You will tap new energies. This is because you are breaking the exhausting habit of eccentricity, and instead are tapping the Source of all energies within, at Centre.

3. You will find yourself approaching the unself-conscious-ness and spontaneity that you enjoyed as a little child. With this difference: then you simply lived from your Home, now you do so with full awareness. But now, as then, you are Space for the people around you to occupy, and by no means one of them. The freedom, the relief, is awesome. Specially if, like me, you had suffered excruciatingly from shame-facedness.

4. In effect, you will perceive that you are *built for loving*. That's to say that you are Empty for the loved one. You vanish in favour of—you give your life for—that one. The feeling follows the vision. Your heart opens, your love starts to flow naturally and freely.

Be patient. Don't demand that these or any other blessings will be apparent at once.

JULY 10

This meditation is safe,
not only because it can't be bungled,
not only because it avoids dependence upon others
on the one hand and self-pride on the other,
but also because it is uncontrived.
There's nothing arbitrary or fanciful about it,
nothing to strain your credulity,
nothing to go wrong,
nothing to set you apart from ordinary people,
nothing special.
It is safe because it is finding out
how matters stand,
not trying to manipulate them.
What could be less dangerous
than ceasing to deceive yourself about your Self,
or more dangerous than not doing so?

This seeing
of the Perfect One
at your core
is instantaneous and perfect
seeing.
To see the Origin at all
is to see It all at once
and as It is.
There are no blurred or partial sightings of
your Origin.

July 12

Only the Awake No-thing
which is the God
who is
perfectly simple
and altogether
present
can be seen at all.
And who but God
can see God?

My life's passion and life-work
have been investigation into
what's so
here,
rather than what's so
there.
In other words, what it's like being oneself,
what one is at centre;
not so much what one looks like
to others over there.
Reality
rather than its many appearances.

JULY 14

What I find difficult and unacceptable really,
is the wishy-washy reliance on words, on concepts,
of so much alleged spirituality.
True spirituality is real,
down to earth,
concrete.
It's coming home
from your appearace
to your reality.
As the Buddha said,
"You won't by going reach that place
where there is the end of suffering.
You'll get it by coming."
We are so good at looking *that* way,
and lousy at looking *this* way.

It isn't that I *could* be wrong about the object out there
but that to some extent I *must* be wrong:
to apprehend it at all is to misapprehend it.
And conversely, it isn't that I'm *likely* to be right
about the bare Subject here
but that I *must* be right:
to see it at all is to see it perfectly,
as it was and is and shall be, for ever and ever,
exactly as all its viewers have seen it and will see it.
Since there is Nothing to see,
I cannot see half of it, nor can I half see it:
this is an all-or-nothing (all-*and*-Nothing) discovery
which removes any anxiety lest my Enlightenment
should be dimmer than yours, or less mature,
or deficient in any way whatsoever.

July 16

My power is weakness.
When I see my total impotence,
even in those nearer regions
where I might seem to exercise some control,
and just let things happen,
then a miracle happens too:
I see that everything is going on
as I want it.

When a thing is seen
from the Source,
it is authorized. It is OK'd.
It could be very painful.
One could be very ill or dying, for that matter,
but when perceived consciously from the Source,
the situation is transformed,
not by a kind of detailed manipulation,
but by viewing it from the Place
that is free of the problem:
from Who one is.

So far from requiring or inducing
a somewhat trancelike state
and temporary retirement from the world
and from people,
this meditation sharpens your appreciation
of what's going on.
You are *more* alive and with it:
Indeed you are the view,
without being lost in it.
It's not when you look at,
but when you overlook,
the Seer
that the seen grows dim and distorted.
Not only the 'outer' world,
but also your 'inner' world
of psychological states,
is obscured when you ignore
the Inmost
which covers and underlies them all.

Surely it is only to be expected that, so long as I fabricate here this central obstruction, this nut of a head, this solid and opaque ball or blob, to serve as the nucleus of my universe, then I am not only hard and hard-faced, but also dense and small-minded, my vision is blocked, my understanding blurred and darkened, my world-picture distorted. With such a spanner thrown in my works, it's a wonder they work at all. And, conversely, when I dissolve this imaginary lump by seeing What's really here, then it is only to be expected that the universe ranged round this simple Clarity (or better, within it) should itself be illuminated and restored to its native order. To be wrongheaded (and to be headed here *is* to be wrong) about the central fact of my world is to be wrong about the rest. Expecting otherwise (as if one could be sane outside and mad inside) is like expecting a watch to go without its mainspring, a tree to flourish without its root, a lamp to shine without wick or oil. How odd that the one spot in the universe which I had systematically overlooked turns out to be the Spot that matters, the more-than-holy Ground which is, precisely, the Solution of all problems and the Fountainhead of all creation!

July 20

This loneliness may suggest lovelessness,
since nobody's left to love.
Paradoxically, it isn't in practice like that at all.
One's love is so total that it leaves
nothing and nobody out in the cold.
One cannot bear not to be all things
everywhere and always:
all alienation is Self-alienation,
all separation is separation from oneself.
It is misery to be confined to this man, this sex,
this nation, this colour, this religion, this planet;
it is misery not to be the company one sees oneself in.
To be Alone is the only joy
which is quite unmixed with sorrow,
the only love which is
untinged with anxiety.

When two-way looking
is persisted in,
the external world
is much more truly and vividly seen
than when it is viewed by itself,
and as if it were the whole story:
as if it were unobserved.
It must be added, nevertheless, that
even this enlightened way of looking
at the world
doesn't begin to perfect
one's knowledge of the world,
whose very nature is that
it can only be inspected piecemeal
and never comprehensively.
Only its Source
is
given all-at-once
and can be viewed unselectively,
with complete objectivity.

My knowledge is ignorance.
In this alert, open, empty receptacle
everything falls into place
without friction or overlapping or left-overs,
and here shines
as itself.

True seers are very distinct people.
Until we see Who we really are,
we tend to be imitative
and not fully individuated,
not our own woman or man
until we are Here universal and impersonal.
Until I see Who I am,
my self-image is built up
on the basis of what is currently approved in society.
But when I see Who I am,
I become, in a certain sense,
a more individuated, separated person.
One *lives* this,
without brooding on it.

July 24

Shut your eyes,
drop memory and imagination,
and notice
whether you have any limits now,
are in any kind of box.

Aren't you more like room:
silence for these sounds to happen in,
space for these passing sensations
of warmth and pressure,
this flow of feelings and thoughts?

Just room or capacity,
but aware of itself now as that!

Yes, Spirit by itself, the Awareness and the I Am and the Being that has to be, that automatically is its sole self from all eternity, is wonderful. But infinitely more wonderful is the Spirit and the Being that doesn't *have* to be, the Awareness that with no help and for no reason continually arises from Unawareness, from Nothing whatsoever, thereby making that Nothing extremely precious as well as indispensable. By virtue of this Nothing it's not *what* Spirit is but *that* it is, which is so breathtakingly adorable. Much the same applies to the arising of our entire Body-Mind (which is none other than the universe) with no help and for no reason, from bare Spirit. What a universe it is, what incredible richness and variety gush tirelessly from this unutterably simple I Am which I am!

JULY 26

Everything I do
is either coming from my human nature,
from my human image
illegitimately and nonsensically superimposed
on the Centre of my life,
or else it is coming from
what is at the Centre of my life,
from Who I am.
The difference between those two kinds of action
doesn't look like much,
but it is very, very deep.
You could sum up the authentic one
as not knowing.
Only don't know.

Tell me what's impossible
after inventing
Oneself.
So I say to the Almighty:
Gosh! That was brilliant!
Staggering!
I think (I'm quite sure)
that the Almighty is as bowled over by it
as I am.
In fact, my being bowled over
is part of His being bowled over.

If you thrill to the inexpressible wonder
of what's beyond Being,
it is *as* Being and *for* Being
that you do so.
And if you are clean bowled over
and miraculously healed
by its incomprehensibility,
it is because incomprehensible
doesn't mean inaccessible,
and mysterious
doesn't mean obscure.
That which in one sense is
the darkest of all secrets
is in another sense
the clearest of the clear,
more obvious than all else,
shining
with its own utmost brilliance.
Reversing your attention,
look now
into the brilliance of your Beyondness,
as well as the beyondness of your Brilliance.

Until I locate for certain my humanness
in its proper place out there
among all those other humans,
until I hold it out there in my bare hands,
there is always the danger
that it will succeed in creeping here
and infecting my Divine Centre,
and will go on to reduce it to a horrendous,
indeed devilish, delusion of grandeur.
It's far from enough that I completely understand
and deeply feel and firmly believe in
the gulf that separates my humanness
from my divinity,
in their absolute incompatibility:
I need also to see it, and see it I do.
How can I express my joy, my relief,
at this seeing-off, this cleansing, this unburdening,
this sure salvation?

July 30

For thousands of years
the wise have been siding with God
and taking this way Home;
and recommending,
with all the eloquence at their command,
this royal road
from human bondage back to divine freedom.
Now, at last,
instead of being told about it by experts,
we are being shown it.
We are invited to *see* our own way through
to God's own country:
the Clear Country we're coming from
and returning to.

Stop believing things
and just have a look,
as if for the first time.

August 1

Second-hand information
is useless when it comes to this crucial question of
one's own Enlightenment.
It's no good relying on hearsay:
on books however sacred, on teachers however revered,
on friends however perceptive and frank.
Even first-hand inspection,
once it has passed over into memory,
will not do.
Only an immediate test,
applied here and now,
will settle the question beyond doubt.
And when I look I see,
at this moment and on this spot,
this non-dual, lucid, simple
Void
which can never be
worked up to, earned, achieved.
Enlightenment has never occurred.
It just is, and there's no escaping it.

Don't imagine that turning *in*
to this imperishable No-thing
is turning *away* from that world
of perishing things,
ceasing to be with it,
involved, caring.
Quite the contrary!
When I overlook the Space I am for them here
I miss-see them.
But when I look 'only' at this Space
I get them thrown in for bonus,
because the Space
is always and absolutely united with its contents.
Looking out,
I get barely half the story;
looking in, I get it all.

August 3

How can I share with you my experience of red. It might be your experience of blue. How can I share with you my pain, or my pleasure: the taste of the apple pie we've had. It's a secret thing. In matters of feeling and sensation, we are really separate and lonesome, aren't we? We are each locked up in a private world, lonely. But there is one thing we can share absolutely, without any shadow of doubt, and that is where we are coming from, who we are and what we are. Why is this utterly shareable? Because there is nothing there to go wrong. The Vision of the One we really are here is a hundred per cent or nothing. Either it exists or it doesn't. If it exists, it's a hundred per cent. Why? Because as St Thomas à Kempis described it, it's a vision of Eternal Clarity: the Country of Everlasting Clearness. I share that with you and with all its citizens. That's sharing. It's the only thing we can really, really share beyond any doubt.

What if your partner wishes to stay short of that Line where you could be absolutely one?

The answer is that you *are* absolutely one, willy-nilly, regardless of whether he or she chooses for the moment to ignore that ever-present truth. So the problem of one-sidedness is, basically, not a real problem at all. Of course, it's good for the two of you consciously to share your descent to the Ground where you are no longer two. All that's essential, however, is that you mind your own business, which at this level *is* the business of your partner and everyone else.

For consider: you are now taking in this printed page. Does the fact that it's not empty-for-you make you any less empty-for-it? Is your enjoyment of a rose dampened by the thought that the sentiment isn't reciprocated? Not in the slightest. The awesome yet self-evident truth is that you can only see Who you really are *as* Who you really are: to wit, as all beings, as the One Seer gazing out of them all. You don't come to that station of true self-awareness and true love (you don't lean back and rest on your Bottom Line) as *somebody*, but as *Nobody-everybody*.

The 'as is' world,
the world as given
before I start mucking about with it
for the purpose of controlling it,
for the purpose of getting power over others,
and so forth
—the world as given to me when I am simple enough
to dare to look at what is presented—
I say, in my experience,
that world is woven of blessings.
It is a world built to
a fabulously beautiful design.

Because I have no will,
my will is done.
Right here,
total impotence
and
total omnipotence
come to the same thing.

AUGUST 7

You are
the sole and final authority
on what it's like
being you,
now,
right where you are.
Nobody else
is in a position to say.

August 8

The whole message that I have,
and which makes it unpalatable to most people is:
you are the authority.
You the reader, the hearer, the workshopee:
you are the authority,
and Douglas is a mere pointer.
What he writes, what he says,
what he does,
is simply to direct you to
the source of all authority:
yourSelf.

August 9

I thrust you back on your own resources.
Everything I say is for testing,
nothing I say is for taking on trust.
The only authority is
Who you are,
not your human nature but
Who you really, really, really are.
All that I am doing is to point to this.
If you find anything that I say
inconsistent with this authority
which is built into you,
which you indeed are,
for God's sake say,
"To hell with it!"

All things are stressed.
Imagining yourself to be
one of those things,
you *take on* its stresses.
But seeing that in fact
you are
empty for that thing,
you *let go* of its stresses.

To get to Heaven, let life *floor* you.
Life is guaranteed to do just that, to let you down:
all the way into the Safety Net
that will never let you down.
Life is guaranteed to disappoint.
But expect *nothing* of the Nothing
that underscores life,
and it cannot disappoint.
Also expect *everything* of it,
and again it cannot disappoint.
It's being so mock-modest in our demands on life,
expecting *something* of it: this or that particular rose,
and with no thorns attached, at that,
which is the stress-maker,
and prevents our enjoyment of the rose-garden.

I'm not saying, mind you,
that a life consciously lived from its
true Centre
will be safe or painless,
easy or consistently joyful.
Real adventure is made of sterner stuff.
You embrace the suffering of the world
no less than its splendour
and its thrill.
The real joy,
the joy that casts no shadow
and knows no variation,
has come through the fire.

August 13

The tendency, when one sees Who one is,
is to be much more aware
of the acts we put on,
of falsities that would otherwise be covered up.
Seeing Who one is
is getting to
the Centre
from which a light shines
on the mind.
One is under fewer illusions
as to one's weaknesses,
one's hang-ups,
one's dubious motives and so on.
This is one of the reasons why,
after many years of seeing,
one seems to be getting worse and worse!
It is because increasingly
a very critical, harsh light
is shone upon the mind
and its subterfuges.

The result of observing only the universe is anxiety. Only
observing the Observer of the universe will put a stop
to your worrying and fussing and scheming. When your
interest is diverted inwards you naturally relax your hold
(your stranglehold) on the outer world. Having withdrawn
your capital and paid it into your own Central Bank (where
it appreciates to infinity), you have nothing to lose out there
and no reason for interfering. You know how to let things
be and work out in their own time. You are in no hurry.
Knowing the Self, you can hardly fail to trust its products.
Whatever occurs is fundamentally agreeable to you. In
Christian terms, you have no will but God's: what you want
is what happens and what happens is what you want. Paradoxically,
your obedience to the nature of things is your rule over them.
Your weakness is in the long run all-powerful. And the secret
of your power over things is that you go to the Source. "Seek
ye first the Kingdom of God, and all these things shall be
added unto you." Seek ye first these things, and even they
shall be taken away.

For the little one, humiliation is hell.
Life keeps putting him down,
and he keeps bouncing back again
by every possible means,
till the irreversible put-down of Death
stops play.
For the Big One,
humiliation is the key to heaven.
It opens the trapdoor
to the stable and well-founded Self-esteem
of the Deathless.

AUGUST 16

Why is the world so troublesome, so frightful? Is it like that by nature, or because we take the easy way of fighting it instead of the difficult way of fitting in with it? We have to find out for ourselves the truth of the sage's demonstration that even in the smallest things the way of non-interference, of giving up all self-will, of 'disappearing', is astonishingly practical, the way that works. Not only in the long run but from moment to moment, consciously getting out of the Light, giving place to whatever happens to be presenting itself in that Light, is astonishingly creative. We do too much and therefore remain ineffectual, we talk far too much and therefore say nothing, we think far, far too much and therefore prevent the facts from speaking for themselves—so say those who know the value of emptiness. It's for us to make our own tests, not—repeat not—by the direct method of trying to be quiet and mindless (it just won't work) but by the indirect method of seeing Who, it seems, was trying to be like that.

August 17

If all we want is to see
Who we really are,
nothing can stop us from doing so
this very moment.
But if our plan is to use
that blessed vision
to buy baskets full of nice feelings
or any other goodies,
we might as well abandon
the very idea of Self-enquiry.

Whereas the ordinary man says,
"My will be done, I hope,"
and the magician says,
"My will be done, I insist,"
the mystic says,
"Thy will be done, I know."
His aim is to submit
with his whole heart
at all times and in all things
to what is,
to God's designs for him
as perfectly displayed
in his present circumstances,
and to leave his future
entirely in God's hands.
The normal man would like to win,
the magician is determined to win,
the mystic is content to surrender.
His attitude could not be more different from theirs.

August 19

In truth,
only Nothing
has room for
Everything.
Only a Nothing
that's awake to its nothingness
is awake to its
Allness.
So long as any part of me
remains unsurrendered
I shall never be Myself.

Until the will
is
surrendered
there is
no
peace.

There is a difference between
suffering that is resisted
and suffering that is
taken on board.
It is in the acceptance of it
that the peace comes.

While seeing
into your Voidness,
seeing that you are Him
now,
notice whether you submit to,
concur in, authorise,
actually *will*
whatever is.
If you now have
no separate will
from His,
aren't you (for the moment, anyhow)
being
Who you truly are?

AUGUST 23

To see
in what is happening to me
at this time
the perfect will of God:
this is a kind of prayer,
a prayer of gratitude.
It is not asking for anything.
It is a surrender
of my little, personal,
private concerns
to Who I really am.

To realise one's true nature
is to realise that one is
the only One that is.
This is a paradoxical combination of
worship, admiration and wonder
for the One,
whilst at the same time realising that
all this is the experience
of the One
by the One:
that one's own Self-awareness
is none other than
God's own Self-awareness.
The realisation that one is
the Alone
means that one is bowled over,
absolutely bowled over
with this achievement of being,
without any help from outside.
And whose achievement?
One's very own, one's very own!
This is the greatest joy in life.
There is nothing to compare with it.

August 25

There is only one:
the Alone.
And there is only one place
where one will find
the Alone:
never in others,
never out there.
Only here.

I locate this
Light Indivisible
right where I am,
plumb in the Centre of this world
as I find it,
nearer than near,
at the heart of the heart of me.
Here is no spark of that
Fire,
but the blazing Furnace itself.
It brooks no rival consciousness.
Awareness comes whole and single.

Look around you for a million years,
ransack the universe,
probe with every instrument into everything,
and nowhere and nowhen will you find
a glimmer of consciousness,
of a will that is not your will,
a hint of a hint of another
I Am.
Never will you find anything or anyone
faintly resembling this
Self-being of yours:
it is absolutely unique, one-off, indescribable.
In God's truth
all of God is right where you are now,
and nowhere else.
I Am is one.
There is no second I Am
to stand in your light,
to put up the feeblest opposition.
All is as you would have it because
you are Who you are.

The only real remedy
for your loneliness
is your Aloneness.
This Aloneness
is the crown of all experience,
the brightest gem in that crown.
Your extremity is God's opportunity:
the opportunity of
the Alone
to be
you.

August 29

One of the consequences of seeing Who one is, is that the mind is no longer felt to be a personal, private, central possession locked up in a brain or a head, but is in fact the world. If one lets one's mind back into the world, the world comes alive again. Seeing the universe as living is seeing the mind as out there, as universal. It is the realisation of the mind as the world or an aspect of the world, and ceasing to divide the world into self/not-self, mind/body, here/there. The whole of what one had stolen from the world—the qualities, the consciousness, the life which one had stolen from the world and encapsulated in a thing called my personality, mind, soul—restoring all this property to the world is the coming to life of the world.

The mind is not central. Your mind is not a personal,
private possession characterising you. It characterises your
objects. Your ideas about objects stick to the objects, and your
ideas and your feelings about things belong to things. This is
really another way of talking about the living universe. The
universe is dead because we killed it. We killed it by taking
the life and the feeling from it and making it our own. This is
altogether false and altogether stupid. It has been a necessary
cultural device, I suppose, for making man more self-aware.
But now it is time that we sent it back to store.

August 31

When you see Who you are,
you see that there is
no place left for the mind
to store things,
no hooks for grappling
thoughts and feelings
to the Centre.
They are centrifugal,
they belong to the world.
Your world becomes
a living world
again.
It comes to life.

The 'form-is-Void' pattern is displayed at all levels. Starting at the top, where it manifests visually as face to no-face, it manifests non-visually lower down as body to no-body and genitals to no-genitals. For provided one attends to what's actually given, the known abolishes the knower and the object ousts the organ that senses it: so that one smells a rose and not a nose, hears drums and not eardrums, touches this page and not fingertips. Genuine love-making is equally simple, equally non-dual and self-effacing, when the lover ceases playing Peeping Tom at his own bedroom keyhole, and becomes an Absentee in respect of all his senses. Imagined symmetry is just as damaging—because as fictitious—below the belt as above. But when it is corrected up there (how easy to disappear for that face!) it is at least well on the way to being corrected below, where symmetry may not be so easy.

September 2

Who is here?
You are the one eyeless Seer,
the one earless Hearer,
the one tongueless Taster.
You are also the one bodiless Lover!
And just as you see the beloved's face
through a conceptual fog while you think
you see it with your eyes,
and muffle the sound of their voice
while you think you hear it with your ears,
so you hardly begin to love their body
while you think you love it with your body.
Only when you submit to being the One
you really are, and they really are,
do you know how to love that body,
and know what sex is really about.
In order to love it is necessary to be God,
for God is love—and, not least, physical love.
In order to be truly one with another
it is necessary to be the One who is that other.

The true goal of sex
is fully to enjoy
—in a profound sense to be enlightened by—
your partner,
and this can only happen
when there's nothing of yourself left
to block and darken the view.
Till you come to this goal,
your union goes unconsummated.

September 4

When making ardent love,
see yourself as absent
in favour of the loved one.
Don't try to feel or understand your absence:
there's Nothing to be felt or understood.
Don't imagine it or think it,
or verbalize the seeing into "Here am I, gone!"
Just look in as well as out.
There are thrills all right,
but no one is here having them.
The thrills are thrilling
because they are genuine:
other-centred and not self-centred,
objective and not subjective.
Sex of this sort is truly enlightening
as well as truly sexual.
Each partner is enlightened by the other.
When partners come together sexually,
they trade bodies.
Each takes in, and takes on, the other.

If we wish to find out
what it's really like
to create the world,
we have only to
desire nothing
and
pay attention.
Total acceptance
is very hard.
It's precisely the opposite
of the lazy indifference
that lets things slide.
It springs from inner strength
and not weakness,
from concentration,
not slackness.

September 6

One of the greatest instruments
of the truth that
God is nearer to me than my humanity
is the mirror,
which takes that human obstruction
out of God's way.
My mirror is a marvellous teacher,
more valuable than
all the scriptures of the world.

My mirror confirms
this wide-openness
right here
where I am.
The very thing which long ago
put a face on me
now relieves me of it.
Now I look in the glass
to see
what I'm not like!

September 8

The whole of my life
and what I have to share with people is:
come back from identifying with
the one in the mirror.
Come back from there to
here,
to your Origin.

To realise this instantaneous
Now,
to live in the present moment,
taking no thought for tomorrow or yesterday,
must be my first concern.
And my second must be
to find in this
Now
all my tomorrows and yesterdays.

SEPTEMBER 10

Time
is in consciousness—
consciousness is not in time.

Seeing Who one is occurs out of time because seeing Who one is is God seeing Who He is, and God doesn't see from half past three until quarter to four. God sees out of time, and my seeing is not Douglas seeing that he is really God, it is God seeing that He is really God. It is out of time and so in that sense one doesn't see all the time or for some of the time, or in time. One sees out of time. Yet there is another sense, of course, in which one can say that one's seeing is intermittent or continuous. That is the common-sense way of talking about it, and we speak of people who flash into their Emptiness and then forget it, for months and months—and then meet a seer, or someone, and flash in again. There is a sense in which this does happen. It is a provisional way of speaking. Even for such people it is really out of time.

September 12

The more steadily I gaze at
the One
that's nearest and clearest,
the more it turns out to be
the dearest,
more me than myself,
the Resource
that never *really* lets me down;
the Wide Awake One
that, though homely and obvious
through and through,
fills me with worship and wonder
at the mystery of
its self-origination,
for no reason and without help or hold-up,
from Nothing Whatever.

Who shall set limits to
the bright blessings
that can arise from
our growing willingness
to trust
what we see,
instead of
what we're told to see?

September 14

Either I am putting my money
on that hopelessly inefficient, dying image
(the one in the mirror)
or I am putting my money on
where I am coming from,
on the Mystery
that has this incredible know-how
and certificate of ability:
that it is.
Now, that is quite a certificate.
And so I trust This.

Things can't be trusted. They pose problems, they change, they perish. Not so this Aware No-thing. It alone can be relied on. It comes up with things—not, it's true, with the things you imagine you want, but with the things you really, really want, the things you need. Is this so surprising? After all, it's from this same unspeakably mysterious No-thing that *all* things emerge for no reason (why should they?), that this wildly improbable universe is now emerging. No mean achievement, this cosmic enterprise ranging from quarks to galaxies, all on the go, all in working order! This is the Thing that your No-thing is getting up to, right where you are. If the power and the expertise behind this Unlimited Liability Corporation, this Business of businesses, can't be counted on, what can? If it lets you get in the red occasionally (and it could) be sure the management has its reasons. If in its service you sometimes go short of this or that (and very likely you will), you suffer no stress on that account. You are well backed.

When I have to make a decision,
which happens all the time,
what I do is refer it back
Here.
In other words,
I see Who I am,
and then I see what I get up to.
See Who you are,
and trust Who you are
to come up with the right answer
at the right time.

The reasons why you should invest at least *some* trust in this, provisionally, and then proceed to put your shirt on it, are three. The first is that many of the now-most-admired members of our species have claimed that (in spite of all appearances to the contrary) they found it altogether reliable, and urged everyone to try it. The second is that, thinking back to the crises in your own life, you may recollect how you drew on far deeper interior levels than those you normally rely on, with impressive results. The third is that the Resource we are recommending is what and where you are coming from, is the Self of yourself, your Origin and own True Nature—and if this can't be relied on you are indeed in a bad way. This which is wholly you, which is more you than *you* are you, yet packs the irresistible power of what's wholly other than you—don't your heart and guts (to say nothing of your head) cry out: "I give myself to This, give myself to my Self, and take the consequences!"?

You won't be sorry.

September 18

I don't mean gritting your teeth and putting on a ghastly smile and saying Yes to all that's happening to you, regardless, as a duty and a discipline. That could lead to harmful repression of your feelings and self-deception—to sweeping your personal garbage, and the world's, under a carpet that doesn't exist. No: see things for what they are, exactly as given in your Emptiness—in this Openness which manifestly has no preferences, no resistances or resentments, no check-list of good and bad things, no categories of beautiful and ugly, acceptable and unacceptable. And see what comes of paying attention to the way you already are. *See how perfectly you are built for this job of willing what is. See how proper and natural it is for you.* And just allow (don't force) the joy to arise, the peace that comes of having nothing to complain about. Given half a chance, it surely will, perhaps much sooner than you imagine possible.

SEPTEMBER 19

No bit of cake
this saying Yes, Yes, Yes.
Or, if it is, this is the saddest cake
ever baked: heaviness itself,
but in the actual taste of it
is a wonderful lightness.
Here, God knows,
is no easy way of life.
But how much harder,
how much more depressing in the long run,
is the life that says No to life!
And how futile, how pathetic!

September 20

See, and see what happens.
This is a working hypothesis for testing
all day and every day:
that the solution of your problem,
no matter *what* it is,
is to see *whose* it is.
Not to understand or feel or think
who has the problem,
but actually to gaze on that Who
and await what comes of the gazing.
This seeing and this waiting
you can always do,
whatever your need.
The rest is out of your hands.

What you now have to do
is to take up His invitation
and go on seeing your way Home to
Him
till your seeing
becomes much more than seeing.
Till it ripens into
trusting wholeheartedly
the only One that's absolutely trustworthy,
and merging wholeheartedly into
the only One
that can really be merged into.

September 22

To every being I say
—not lightly but with all my heart—
here in the depths of me, as Who I really, really am,
I am the One you really, really are.
Though we may belong to vastly different regions and eras,
wear vastly different faces,
enjoy vastly different experiences of the world,
all these are peripheral matters,
matters of accident and time and content,
and are transcended
in the one central, timeless Container and Essence
in which I'm aware of myself
as you, and you, and you, *ad infinitum*.
The barriers are down,
our wounds are healed,
and we are well again because we are One again.

Only in this Root, only as this Root,
are we all One and the Same for ever.
This meditation infallibly unites you
with all creatures
at the one Spot where all converge,
where we are at last wholly relieved
of those manifest peculiarities
and hidden feelings and thoughts
which distinguish and part us from one another.
The Void, just because It really is void,
is identical in all beings everywhere and at all times.
If It could be experienced as loving in me,
bright in you, and specially empty in him,
It would only serve to thrust us still further apart.
But in fact you are him and me,
without the slightest doubt or anxiety,
directly you find the Spot
where there's Nothing to come between us.

Seeing Who you are is seeing that you are all beings.
The principle is established,
whether consciously or semi-consciously,
that your commitment to them is infinite;
that you are One with every sentient being,
whether it is a spider,
or a visitor from a galaxy far away,
or the people in your own house,
or the people you find especially trying or stupid.
Your involvement with them is basically total,
for the simple reason that intrinsically you are that person,
you are that strange being,
you are that horrible monster,
and there are in the last resort no horrible monsters.
This means that in fact one's behaviour after seeing
is more altruistic, more giving,
though it may be more shocking than before.

This meditation doesn't preclude,
and need not interfere with,
any other kind of meditation,
such as 'sitting meditation',
which you may find helpful.
What it does rule out
is meditation which assumes
the meditator isn't already at Home.

SEPTEMBER 26

Truly I forget in what my wealth
and true grandeur lie,
and how inexhaustible they are,
and how my title to them
is my absolute poverty.
Plunging head-first
into the sea of nothingness,
I find there untold treasure.

There remains what is perhaps
the greatest illusion of all—the illusion that,
if you are a mere person with a head,
a finite thing bounded by other finite things,
so, even more certainly is your neighbour.
And consequently he is there to be used
like any other thing.
But once you really awake to your own headlessness,
you cannot stop there,
but must wake to mine and every creature's.
Putting yourself at my centre,
you see me as I am
—boundless and deathless—
because I am the habitation of the One
who is boundless and deathless,
and in the last resort
there is only the One.

September 28

That little one, poor fellow, has to live with two conflicting pieces of knowledge—the deep conviction that all the world is his in reality, and the superficial certainty that almost none of it is his in practice. Result: greed. He's driven to amass around himself all manner of possessions—tokens of his infinite wealth—regardless of how trivial and superfluous and plain cock-eyed they may be. Regardless of the fact that these possessions, taken together, make such demands on him that they come to possess him. Regardless of the fact that only the moment of getting is pleasure: before that is the pain of not having, after that the pain of not having. The Big One is relieved of both pains. He's so Big there's nothing left to get and have. He doesn't own a thing. You name it, he is it. As No-thing whatever he's capacious of all things, and is satisfied.

By coming to look at ourselves from outside, we lost this treasure, we lost this wealth, and we spend the rest of our lives—alas, many of us—trying to get back a part of our lost heritage. I really do believe that when we see who we really are, we don't crave unnecessary objects—which are put there, simply, I think, for us to get some symbol or token of our lost treasure. When the world is yours, why go for a million dollars? Chicken-feed! Pathetic!

September 30

To the extent that I stay centred
in the perfection of the New Man,
of my True Nature as First Person Singular,
the manifold imperfections of the old man are mitigated.
To the extent that I live from the values of this New Man
—unconditional love, no power over others,
no turning one's back on them,
the acceptance of humiliation, and so forth—
to that extent the contrasting values of that old man
become less and less heavy
and humourless and troublesome,
and more and more amenable
and realistic and healthy.
In a word, more natural.

When my attention is centred
primarily upon
the One
who is attending here,
and only incidentally upon the world
that confronts me,
the world is made marvellous in me.
Then the great surprise,
the most astounding fact of all,
isn't *what* the Cosmos is but
that it is;
not the infinitely varied products *there*
but their simple Origin *here*.

October 2

The little one's knowledge
is the ending of wonder;
the Big One's knowledge
is the beginning of wonder.
The little one is heady and knowing and smart:
he'll buy knowledge
at the expense of mystery every time,
and sooner or later it gives him
a splitting headache.
The Big One buys mystery
at the expense of knowledge
till all that's left is
the Mystery itself,
the Perfectly-known-as-unknowable-Source
that is the cure
of all the headaches it gives rise to.

Paradoxically,
I'm forever returning
to the Place I never left.
And Heaven help me
if I kid myself that I've travelled
that road often enough,
thank you very much,
and it's high time
I settled down comfortably,
at the comfortable end of it.

OCTOBER 4

I certainly don't find myself
on the brink of a bottomless abyss,
trying to make up my mind
whether to let go and take that dreadful plunge.
I'm already clear of the brink
and free-falling,
and have never been otherwise.
To see this,
all I have to do is look for myself,
and fail to find myself,
and find instead
the treasure that has no name
in the well
at the world's end.

When we are at our best are we not thankful
that this glorious and terrible Reality
is just what it is?
The fact that it is mysterious beyond telling
and altogether unlike our design for it—
this is surely the very thing that makes it so adorable.
In Hell we know and are known only too well,
and are all expert theologians and psychologists;
but in Heaven we never begin to recover
from our astonishment at one another,
and therefore boredom is unknown.
Knowledge that is only knowledge
is the very abyss of ignorance.

October 6

My finest and most thrilling discovery is that,
because all my roots are in the Undiscoverable,
I also am undiscoverable:
I will not bear inspection,
and can never make head or tail of myself.
Self-knowledge is the smouldering wick that is left
after the light of wonder has been put out.
Once the universe becomes credible,
once I seriously suppose I know
a thing or two about myself,
then I have sunk back
into the stupor of the half-dead.

It all boils down to this simple thing:
what am I in my own experience
at this time?
What am I
looking out of?
Because that's real, that's my reality,
as distinct from my appearance for you.

October 8

Trusting Who I really am
means that when I have to act,
I'm not acting from the resources
of that little one in the mirror,
but from the resources of the
I Am
this side of the mirror.
There's no in-between.

This is a very good bargain:
trading one tiny thing in the universe
for the whole darn lot.
It's so profitable!
To exchange
this one mortal non-OK thing
for the whole world!

OCTOBER 10

What this means in practice is that
every time I arrive here
is a 'first time',
because in fact it's out of time.
It means that my disappearing
in your favour
gets more and more surprising,
my single eye opens wider and wider
with amazement,
and I shall never get used to
how my Renault Clio
stirs the world
as if it were a bowl of porridge.

It is a marvellous thing to realise,
an essential thing to realise,
that as human beings we are a washout,
that everything is lost,
the whole situation has gone to pot.
Then we rely only on Who we are.
We have to die
before
God can live in us.

October 12

What an instant resource
we have right here,
as awesome as it is intimate
and as mysterious as it is available!
What a medicine against death,
what an everlasting refuge
lies at our very heart,
visibly expanding to take in
and take care of
everything!
And given
Now
in its fullness and depth,
however incompetent or undeserving
we may be,
whatever our mood
and just when we need it most!

What is true Enlightenment
but just this facing the facts,
in all honesty and simplicity?
It is going by what one clearly sees
for oneself
and no longer by
what one is told or imagines.
It is plucking up courage
to fit the world to one's perceptions
instead of one's perceptions to the world.
It is taking seriously
whatever is clearly presented
without trying to improve upon it
or explain it away.

OCTOBER 14

In one's heart
one has always known that
one is infinite,
all-inclusive,
the one who overcomes the world.
Who is here?
There's only one answer that
rings true and satisfies and is quite final:
the one here
is
the Immense,
the All.

October 15

The one here is the solution
of all the problems that proliferate out there,
in the country of problems.
They are wholly resolved
by discriminating between this central region
which is visibly clear of problems
(and everything else)
and the surrounding country
where no problem is ever cleared up.

October 16

It is impossible steadily to observe
this central Gap or Hiatus
without observing also that
this is precisely what one is:
No-thing dependent upon nothing,
truly free from everything.
It isn't a matter of achieving this state,
but of accepting it as unalterable fact.
One has no choice here.
Detachment is the mark of this First Person,
as attachment is the mark of that third person.
The world runs like water off one's back
while he is soaked to the bone.

So long as I keep up the pretence that
this one is rather like the others,
there is no reason for wonder.
But when I clearly see what it's like here,
and consciously am this total emptiness
(which nevertheless is very much alive to itself)
then this self-seeing is mixed with astonishment.
'So What?' becomes 'Dumbfounded!';
and so far from the surprise wearing off,
it grows with cultivation.

OCTOBER 18

The only way not to be lost
in the crowd
is
to *be* the crowd.

October 19

Every day, one takes oneself
—the fact of one's actually having happened—
less for granted.
Not *what* one is,
but *that* one is:
this is ever more fascinating;
and it is inseparable from
that final irregularity,
that virtual impossibility:
the fact that there is anything whatever.

October 20

That This should have contrived
Its own being,
engineered Its own emergence,
without reason or cause or any assistance,
out of mere inane nothingness;
that It should possess the knack
of pulling Itself up
by its own astonishing bootstraps
out of the ocean of non-being:
what success, what audacity,
what splendour!
After this impossible feat,
nothing is impossible
and everything is mystery,
unknowable,
inexplicable.

Just as creative thinking
comes from no-thinking,
from clear-headedness
(the head, too, cleared away),
and just as effective action
comes from no-action,
from interior stillness,
so does real feeling come from no-feeling,
from total detachment and impassivity
aware of itself as such.

October 22

When I attend carefully to
what lies right here
at the storm-centre of the universe,
I find perfect calm.
The middle of the world
has quietly dropped out.
But really it never had a middle,
and was always hollow, coreless.
This Hub
of the ever-turning cosmic wheel
has never been anything but
still, idle and vacant.

I interfere with nothing out there,
and nothing out there interferes with me.
I have nothing to do,
and yet I see all doing as proceeding from here.
I find no need to be anything,
and yet I see all being as contained here:
in this unique Gap,
this wonderful Hiatus,
which turns out to be
the fountain of continual creation.

October 24

Here, indeed, is no ordinary spot:
no place on the map, in the cosmos,
is anything like it.
This still Centre is the one spot
where energy is actually discovered
welling up out of Nothing.
All the irresistible torrents
which swirl and roar through every other place
rise silently in this Place,
never ruffling its
perfect calm.

For this First Person
there is neither far nor near
(I don't see distance)
and all are dear.
All are myself,
inasmuch as I have nothing
to keep them off with:
my nothingness and their somethingness
unite absolutely.
Every one of them is needed
to fill this great empty
Heart of mine.

October 26

I always come as an astonishment to myself,
and can never begin to take myself for granted.
I learn nothing about myself,
never get used to myself
(what is there to learn about and get used to?)
and am always introducing myself to myself,
bowing with profound respect
and the keenest delight
(not unmixed with amusement)
at this strange meeting.
And this is no formality: I am truly brand new,
without history, inheritance
or continuity of any kind.
Every moment sees me starting from scratch.

How could I own the stars,
except by being the space
in which they shine;
or own anything,
except by letting it
replace me?

OCTOBER 28

Everything short of the Whole
is too small to be free.
Only the Whole is self-contained,
subject to no outside influences,
complete,
and quite alone.
And when I claim to be free
I am really claiming
—with what effrontery!—
to be the Whole.

What is it like, how does it feel,
to be this lonely one,
absolutely on my own?
It's to feel lightsome and unconcerned,
to breathe a great sigh of relief.
It's to enjoy the sweet relaxation of
having no external authority
to please and make up to.
It's to have won through,
to be victorious over the world,
and at peace at last.
It's to have settled final accounts
with death and evil,
to have nothing to lose or gain,
and to be desireless.
And, incidentally,
it's to hold no very high opinion of oneself,
no low opinion, no opinion at all,
seeing that no standards apply to
this incomparable one.

October 30

Only when I see my aloneness
am I incapable of boredom.
I adore my own company
and every moment of it is a delight.
And *only* when there's not a particle
left outside me
has all possibility of terror gone:
one little thing lost to me,
a single refugee from my embrace,
and I'm threatened, I'm lost.
It's only when I am all things
and no differences remain,
that I'm safe Home,
comfortable
and easy.

Here you are deader than dead.
Not till you see this clearly
and accept it deeply,
are you empty enough,
are you burst wide open enough,
to be flooded with
the resurrection life
that is the life
of the whole world.
When you find, beyond all doubt,
that you are this dreadful Waste Land,
then you find there the Holy Grail,
already flooding you to overflowing
with its living water.

November 1

Everything perishes.
If you don't want to perish,
go
where there isn't anything
to perish.
Then you find that
you are there already.
This does put paid to
the fear of death.

It's the old, old story:
die to live.
Give your life.
The way to have your life is to give it up,
dying into the new life:
the death of the little one
and the birth of the Big One.

NOVEMBER 3

What is nothing but vacancy
for everything
is at once too mean
and too great to die:
it could not be more permanently dead
than it is in itself,
or more permanently alive
than it is in its objects.

My life's work is
to find out for myself
what this spot is like,
and who lives here,
right now.
To do this it is essential to be deaf
to all the voices out there
telling me what it looks like here:
as if they could know,
or had any right to pronounce
on such a question,
or were in any position to do so!

November 5

Let me only be honest
and see and be who I am,
and cease playing third person,
and observe the result,
and trust that result.
Then I discover that
I am not inhabiting
the same old world as before.
Though the bare data are
in some sense just the same,
every slightest thing is profoundly altered.
And suffusing them all
is this indescribable peace.

If I'm realistic about what it's like here
I shall spontaneously live
according to the law of selfless love;
and I shall live this life
from moment to moment
in perfect trust,
unconcerned about tomorrow.
I see that this is the only life I'm built for,
and that only this First Person
is unsubstantial enough
to filter through the needle-eye gate
that leads to it.

November 7

Clearly *seeing* this inner Brilliance
(*thinking* it is no good,
and even feeling it is far from good enough)
roots out one's fundamental anxiety.
The Heart of all things is visibly sound,
and this is enough.
Now the outward aspects of things
can be accepted fearlessly
and processed efficiently:
from the Void that produces them.

The First Person is God.
The One on *this* side of the mirror
and on *this* side of everything seen,
the One here who sees without eyes
and hears without ears,
the One here who exclaims
—"I Am! I've actually occurred!"—
this One is God.

November 9

What does it feel like to be Him?
One can say that only this is Home;
only this total identity satisfies;
that to be saved is to *be* Him;
that this Homecoming
is perfectly natural to the First Person
who has never really left Home anyway.
But such talk is, strictly, inadmissible.
Who is this First Person addressing but
this First Person?
There are conversations
which can only be concluded
wordlessly
and in private.

What is the truly First Person,
game-free, spiritual life?
Instead of training, enjoyment.
Instead of working for the future,
realisation of what is present to perfection,
with no other end in view.
Instead of indoctrination,
the inexhaustible adventure of self-discovery.
Instead of psychological improvement
or spiritual development, total evacuation now,
the surrender of all ambitions and claims.

This,
the freely given present,
is sufficient.
Concerned only with this,
one finds the days, months, years
slipping by almost unnoticed,
and every day is a good day.

Once I go into the matter thoroughly,
for myself and wholeheartedly,
I find I can doubt everything
but this supreme Certainty,
this Conviction
which makes all other convictions
seem mere notions,
this bed-rock Certainty
that remains unshaken
when every opinion is shattered.
I am the One,
with no separate being or existence.
Truly this is all I know.
Everything else was fantasy.

November 13

What is needed
isn't more spiritual or mental discipline,
or study, or prolonged and systematic meditation,
or any working up of states,
but simple honesty, courage, faith,
and single-mindedness:
the honesty to see what there is to see
without editing it,
the courage to take it seriously,
the faith to act on it,
and the single-mindedness
just to go on being quietly Oneself.
Then there are no more problems.

I find that whenever I have the grace
and the good sense
to submit
to what is freely presented
at this moment,
without trying to improve upon it,
the Clear Light of What-I-Am
(and therefore what everything else is)
blazes forth.

November 15

In order for the One
who is All
to take up residence
here at my Centre,
that Centre
must be quite empty
of all things.

It is impossible
for one
not to vanish in favour of
the person one is addressing:
impossible not to give
one's very life for that person.
Confrontation
is a thundering great lie.

One's seeing needs to be practised and stabilised,
till it goes on all the while.
Actually, 'practised' is misleading:
'enjoyed' is nearer the mark,
because seeing is so very easy,
natural, and agreeable.
All the same, it can be neglected,
and total dedication is indispensable.
Normally, it will take years of
more-or-less deliberate seeing
before seeing becomes quite automatic,
in all the circumstances of daily life.
In the end, there will be no occasions
which are unfavourable to Self-seeing.

Here, one says "I Am!"
and that is enough.
Not *how* I am or *what* I am,
but *that* I am:
not what I look like, or embrace, or do,
but the simple and astounding fact that
I Alone Am:
this incredible achievement of having,
without help or reason or cause,
raised Myself out of the chaos of
non-existence and nullity into
Being.
This alone is true spiritual knowledge:
the knowledge of the unknowable Mystery,
which is the Self's own wonder at Itself.

November 19

The only way to *see* the Self
is to be interested enough just to look,
once and for all,
at the Spot one occupies.
And the only way to *be* the Self
is to submit,
once and for all,
to the experience of Aloneness.

When I do see What I really am here to myself,
I find myself ceasing to care how I look over there.
All that interests me now is what I actually find
instead of what I imagine.
I take myself exactly as given
—as mere capacity or empty room—
and others exactly as given:
as filling this room with their fascinating shapes
and colours and movements and speech.
Now my new-found attention to
and enjoyment of
these others,
along with my lack of anxiety about myself,
ensure that my responses shall be
much more sensitive,
swift, spontaneous,
and (in the long run) appropriate.
No doubt the others are better served now,
but how I'm going down with them
is none of my business. My business is
what impression they are making here,
and upon Whom.

When have I ever trusted
the Nature of things
too much,
or been too open to it?
What lets me down is not how things are,
but what I do to them.

Look and see.

This wonder of wonders
is by far
the most precious gift you possess.

When I look
here,
and dare to be my own authority,
and really see what's going on,
I find everything
is really the opposite
of what I've been told.
This is Good News,
because what one discovers is
a sheer marvel,
a joy.
It puts things right.

I've never been
face to face
with anybody.
It's always been
*face to spac*e.
In other words, the wonderful truth,
God's truth,
is that we are built for loving.

NOVEMBER 25

The joke is we never left home really.
Another joke is:
everybody's doing it right.
I'm not saying you've got to reform yourself.
Maybe that's desirable,
but I'm saying
the real reform is to wake up to
your incredible, central blessedness,
at this moment.
Then see what else needs doing.

This is not a mystical experience,
it's not a peak experience,
because you can't regain peak experiences.
They are just one-off things. You can't lay them on.
But this one you can.
You can always come back to it.
It's a 'valley' experience.
It has nothing to do with feeling—it is a matter of fact.
You can always come back to this,
however dim or dark your mood.
It is simple, available all the time.
You can count on it.
It's nothing to do with excitement and euphoria.
It is essentially a cool thing.
But what does this cool thing conceal?
What does it offer us?
It offers us love, really:
the love behind the world.

It's a case of wanting what you get,
and not of getting what you want.
This is the assimilation of your will
to the will of God.
Dante again:
His will
(or I'd say Her will nowadays)
His will is our peace.

The funny thing is,
when we stop this compulsive urge
to change everything,
that is the biggest change of all.
Acceptance:
saying Yes to what is happening to us.
De Caussade, a great, great man said:
"If we will see in the present moment
God's perfect will for us
(in our situation, at this moment)
we will find in it all our heart could desire."
Now it's a big claim.
It's for testing, isn't it?
It's not for believing, it's for testing.

November 29

Nothing could be more vivid,
immediate, practical and handy
than this brilliant Void
which I am,
and in which there is no room for death.

NOVEMBER 30

All things are transfigured,
aglow with morning splendour,
now they are *where* they have always been anyway:
over there
and not here.

December 1

Enlightenment is to be found
nowhere but
here,
at no time but
now.

DECEMBER 2

If such adjectives as
Godlike, divine, unconditioned, perfect, real,
apply anywhere at all,
they apply here and only here.
Nowhere but on this spot can I find Him,
and here I find Him without coverings,
totally manifest.
(If I don't care for the word 'God',
I can substitute Atman, Buddha-nature,
the Self, the One, the Void, or what I like.
There are many names for This,
for the Nameless which, precisely because
it is so real and vivid in experience,
cannot be named or thought about.)

December 3

Thought itself supplies many good reasons
why thought is out of place here,
in this central, First Person country,
the land of the present.
For example, thought takes time,
is never all of it contained
in one moment of its on-going process,
is always looking to the past and the future,
is (in short) time-ridden;
whereas this spot is only now
and free of time.

What is the practical answer
to the practical problem set by the Sages:
the problem of how to stop one's thinking
in order to become Enlightened?
Instead of stopping thought,
I have only to place it,
out there in its own place.
Instead of rejecting thoughts,
I have only to authorise them,
where they are perfectly in order.
Instead of making enormous efforts
to improve the situation,
I have only to see that it is all right
and everything is already achieved.
No thought can ever come quite Home
or penetrate this Clear Country.
All I must do, then, is stay at Home.
And this is so easy once I see
what this wonderful Home is like.
It takes no practice to be a real Home-lover.

December 5

Somehow it has come off:
this very special enterprise,
this incredible feat of having,
without any help or reason or cause,
raised Oneself out of non-existence
into glorious Actuality.
This is at once the highest knowledge
and the deepest ignorance:
the Self's own wonder at Itself,
the divine surprise,
the Mystery revelling in the Mystery.

The awesome truth is that
this Central No-thing
is not only the ineffable Source
of all those peripheral things,
but far more brilliantly on display
than any of them.
Only This can be perfectly seen
because only This
is
perfectly simple!

December 7

That great poet and saint St. John of the Cross
tells me that to be all things
I must be nothing,
but I don't have to take his word for it.
I can always check this astounding fact,
whatever my mood or activity of the moment,
just by taking a look at
what I'm looking out of
right here.

The meaning and purpose of my life
is conscious union with its Divine Source.
Of course I'm a human being still,
but it's way off-Centre
and peripheral to the true me by a metre,
more or less.
Here at my Centre
is the Home of the One I really am,
of the One who is All.

December 9

Let us have the courtesy
and good sense
to let God be God at the Centre
and humans be human off-Centre.
Then God is Godlike
and humans are humane.

'I am what I look like'
is hell.
You can't live from that.
What I look like is dying.
What I am isn't.

December 11

The moment you think that
there must be something else,
and that seeing your total Emptiness
is not enough,
then you have stopped seeing it
and are thoroughly unenlightened.
But once you have really looked
into the place you occupy
(and found you don't occupy it!)
you can always drop thinking
and look in again,
at will.
The thing is then to will to look
more and more often,
till you see all the while
What you are.

Though it is a useful preparation,
no amount of understanding the Self
will ever build up to seeing the Self.
And for a very good reason:
seeing This is quite incompatible with
thinking about This,
and is a much simpler
and more direct experience.
Instead of *knowing* that right here,
on the Spot one occupies,
is this brilliant Clarity
without so much as a speck of body-mind,
one actually *sees* this Clarity,
and sees it more sharply and convincingly
than one sees anything else whatever.
The Self here enjoys itself
as perfectly lucid, transparent, obvious.

December 13

How does it feel to be
the only One,
the Alone,
the Origin,
the self-generating Self?
To be
this unthinkable mystery?
To celebrate not *what* I am but *that* I am,
since there is no reason for anything to be at all?
Somehow, inconceivably,
I arrange my own existence.
It's impossible!
But who is now feeling
this incomparable wonder?
How could a person begin to do so?
Who but the Self knows this joy?
To whom but the Self could it come so naturally?

DECEMBER 14

In workshops, I'm constantly finding people who say, "Well, I had the Vision in a previous workshop, but then I lost it." This is absurd. Once you've seen it, you know where to look, how to look, what to look for. You've no excuse for neglecting or overlooking it. In fact, they're not saying they've lost it. They're saying they've lost the feeling of it, they've lost the euphoria, they've lost the joy of it or the initial, emotional thrust of it. Of course, that will go. Yesterday afternoon, there was a lady who was obviously in ecstasy about it. I said to her, "It will go." The Vision won't go, but the ecstasy will.

DECEMBER 15

Something has happened to you
which is extremely precious
and astonishing,
and I think very much overlooked
and disregarded,
some enormous privilege
which you are enjoying,
and I am enjoying,
and that is:
one has actually happened.
One has
occurred!

December 16

Who you really are,
at centre,
your inmost nature,
your awareness itself,
is not a product of the world:
it is the origin of the world.

December 17

It is the mystery
behind this fabulous universe:
you are not a little bit of that divine fire,
not a spark of that divine fire
but the fire itself,
all of it present in you,
in what you are looking out of,
nearer to you than the one in your mirror,
nearer to you than everything else.
Who you are,
what you really are,
is none other than that,
in full strength
and flourishing in good nick!

What I experience
depends upon many things:
upon the state of
my physical and chemical layers,
my brain, my body, my world,
and ultimately upon the whole of things.
That I experience
depends upon No-thing.
Awareness is the function of
– it is –
this unbounded Emptiness.

December 19

One important point we must make here
is that we are not trusting it
to give us what we currently fancy.
We are trusting it
to give us what we deeply, profoundly need.
That's different.
It doesn't give you what you want.

This is not getting what you want,
it's wanting what you get.
That seems supine and unadventurous, but it isn't.
When we live from the truth of Who we are
and stay centred,
we shall find that what we really want
is what we really get,
and that mercy and blessings flood us
when we tell the truth.
We are built for loving, for a start.
We are immortal,
because there's nothing here to die.
Everything that the heart could desire,
plus everything else,
is available now.
Come on, test it!

December 21

Your true self is full of the whole world, isn't it?
Looked at in this inward direction,
why it is plain, like soil really.
Looked at in that outward direction,
the bloom of the world!
And it's so beautiful.
The amazing thing is that
we are so much more fortunate
than we had ever suspected, aren't we?
We are in luck: God's luck.
The lucky one!
Lucky strike!
We struck lucky!

It has to be simple to be effective.
All those decorative experiences,
those mystical experiences,
are marvellous,
but you want something to come back to
that is plain,
ordinary, available.
Here it is.

December 23

This is power,
because if you are saying
Yes
to the will of God,
things happen as you will.
As you wish.
So it is a position of power.
Paradoxically,
surrender of the will
is the acquisition of the real will.

What keeps me on the ball,
at least coming back and back and back,
is curiosity.
I find it such fun.
It's not a solemn old thing.
New discoveries, new things, are coming up.
It's so exciting and so delightful.
As far as I'm concerned,
the name of the game is
discovery, adventure.
Everything comes out differently
from what it had been advertised to be!
It's discovery all along the line.
This is great fun.
Extraordinary revelations are available,
once you get to the heart of the matter.
It's always new,
always coming up with new stuff.
This is so interesting, isn't it?

December 25

It's not a miracle that is happening
somewhere else.
It's taking place
right Here.
You are a magician
bringing yourself out of this hat of
Non-Being,
and you haven't a clue
how you are doing it.
I take my stand
on that
which I cannot understand.

December 26

I'm going to try to make
every remaining day of my life
a Yes day.
Only say Yes
and all shall be well.

December 27

Rest assured
that one moment
of seeing yourself as Empty-for-all
affects all profoundly.
Your best contribution to the future
isn't what you say,
or even what you work for,
but what you *are* now.
Nothing is so catching as
this well-founded freedom from stress,
this impersonal serenity
that must embrace all persons.

The seeing itself is a very precise,
unmistakable,
all-or-nothing experience,
renewable at will.
One cannot half see one's facelessness,
nor can one see half of it.
Either one does or one doesn't see
one's Original Face,
and to doubt the validity of one's seeing is
(while it lasts)
quite impossible.

December 29

There is that supreme irregularity:
the fact that anything exists at all.
Most unnaturally,
there is not just Nothing.
How adroit of It to happen!
How deserving of our congratulations
It is
for having arranged
its quite impossible existence!
After that, what are
a few billion universes more or less?
What impossibilities may not
It or He have up His sleeve?
And what may I not be in Him?

I am sure that God,
bless her heart,
is thrilled by the universe,
but I think her chief joy,
her chief surprise and wonder,
is wonder at
her own self-origination,
for no reason
and with no help:
the mystery of Nothingness,
unaware of itself,
achieving Awareness,
Non-Being flipping over into Being.
And she doesn't know how she does it!
She couldn't know how she does it!
When we enjoy this, it is worship.

December 31

I am grateful
for the miracle of Being.
In the last resort
one is grateful and astounded
that there isn't just nothing,
isn't just a dark night of non-existence.

DOUGLAS HARDING

Douglas Harding (1909—2007) was tremendously creative in the service of our true self. He wrote many books and articles, invented the headless way experiments, designed the Youniverse Explorer model, and gave many workshops world-wide. Dedicating his long life to being aware of, and sharing the experience and meaning of, 'who we really are', he transmitted this View to thousands of people.

For more information about Douglas Harding and 'seeing who you really are', visit headless.org

BOOKS BY DOUGLAS HARDING

Short Stories
The Meaning And Beauty Of The Artificial
How Briggs Died
The Melwold Mystery
An Unconventional Portrait Of Yourself
The Hierarchy Of Heaven And Earth (original full version)
The Hierarchy Of Heaven And Earth (condensed version)
Visible Gods
On Having No Head
Religions Of The World
The Face Game
The Science Of The First Person
The Hidden Gospel
Journey To The Centre Of The Youniverse
The Little Book Of Life And Death
Head Off Stress
The Trial Of The Man Who Said He Was God
Look For Yourself
The Spectre In The Lake
Face To No-Face
To Be And Not To Be
Open To The Source
The Turning Point
Just One Who Sees
As I See It

REFERENCES

1. TMG 59
2. LFY 236
3. FG 81
4. FTNF 91
5. VI Pt 2
6. LW
7. AISI 537
8. HHE 257
9. HOS 246
10. HOS 280
11. LFY 263
12 LBLD 117
13. SWYRA 146
14. S1P 56
15. OHNHV
16. Int 1977
17. LBLD 110
18. LBLD 110
19 FTNF 101
20. TMG 393
21. S1P 16
22. Int 1977
23. TMG 59
24. LBLD 24
25. Int 1977
26. LFY 31
27. HHE 236
28. AISI 111
29. LFY 186
30. HOS 113
31. LBLD 110
32. TP 27
33. LBLD 78
34. FTNF 61
35. FTNF 61
36. FTNF 61
37. FTNF 62
38. SWYRA 32
39. SWYRA 33
40. SWYRA 33
41. FTNF 127
42. AISI 116
43. TMG 22
44. TMG 24
45. SWYRA 119

46. HOS 210
47. LBLD 23
48. VI Pt 3
49. VI Pt 3
50. HOS 130
51. S1P 84
52. S1P 85
53. S1P 85
54. TBNTB 134
55. S1P 84
56. HOS 279
57. HHE 257
58. HOS 274
59. SWYRA 42
60. VI Pt 4
61. LFY 24
62. FTNF 29
63. Int 1977
64. FTNF 68
65. HHE 143
66. Int 1977
67. HHE 58
68. HHE 129
69. FTNF 32
70. HHE 123
71. VI Pt 4
72. VI Pt 4
73. VI Pt 4
74. HOS 280
75. HOS 280
76. LBLD 111
77. HOS 280
78. HOS 124
79. LFY 82
80. TMG 176
81. VI Pt 2
82. OHNHV
83. TP 32
84. FTNF 78
85. FTNF 23
86. LFY 320
87. FTNF 19
88. VI Pt 3
89. SWYRA 56
90. HOS 128

91. Int 1977
92. SWYRA 119
93. SWYRA 101
94. SWYRA 101
95. HHE 81
96. HOS 273
97. TP 22
98. HHE 118
99. VI Pt 4
100. TMG 239
101. TMG 26
102. FTNF 105
103. Int 1977
104. FTNF 105
105. S1P 83
106. S1P 84
107. TMG 144
108. SWYRA 56
109. Int 1977
110. LFY 259
111. Int 1977
112. SWYRA 56
113. HOS 209
114. S1P 38
115. LFY 203
116. FTNF 120
117. FTNF 192
118. S1P 81
119. TMG 144
120. S1P 68
121. FTNF 162
122. FTNF 195
123. SWYRA 119
124. OHNH 10
125. TP 24
126. HHE 18
127. LFY 288
128. HW19 21
129. SWYRA 147
130. SWYRA 58
131. LFY 72
132. TMG 33
133. HOS 198
134. FTNF 32
135. VI Pt 2

136. SWYRA 143
137. LFY 287
138. LFY 287
139. TMG 208
140. LFY 233
141. TMG 393
142. LBLD 116
143. Int 1977
144. LBLD 80
145. HOS 17
146. HOS 302
147. HOS 302
148. LFY 256
149. LFY 257
150. LFY 299
151. Int 1977
152. S1P 88
153. S1P 88
154. TMG 259
155. SWYRA 33
156. SWYRA 120
157. VI Pt 3
158. Int 1977
159. SWYRA 146
160. SWYRA 146
161. ML
162. HOS 173
163. VI Pt 3
164. OHNHV
165. SWYRA 163
166. SWYRA 163
167. SWYRA 163
168. HOS 128
169. LFY 271
170. LFY 271
171. LBLD 109
172. OHNHV
173. OHNHV
174. SWYRA 33
175. FTNF 40
176. TBNTB 125
177. LFY 289
178. HOS 214
179. FG 347
180. TBNTB 71

181. S1P 40
182. HOS 188
183. LFY 94
184. OHNHV
185. OHNHV
186. OHNHV
187. HOS 123
188. HOS 178
189. S1P 75
190. TMG 27
191. LFY 213
192. SWYRA 41
193. TBNTB 165
194. TBNTB 166
195. RO
196. VI Pt 3
197. S1P 25
198. FG 273
199. FTNF 152
200. SWYRA 32
201. S1P 41
202. FG 269
203. S1P 22
204. FG 271
205. FTNF 82
206. YT
207. LFY 263
208. FTNF 131
209. VI Pt 4
210. HOS 295
211. TBNT 82
212. TMG 24
213. OHNHV
214. FG 339
215. LBLD 146
216. VI Pt 3
217. HOS 225
218. ML
219. TBTB 126
220. OHNHV
221. Int 1977
222. Int 1977
223. HOS 26
224. HOS 231
225. TBNB 154

226. Int 1977
227. LFY 32
228. TMG 395
229. LFY 33
230. LFY 35
231. LFY 227
232. LFY 330
233. FTNF 120
234. FTNF 123
235. SWYRA 89
236. SW
237. Int 1977
238. Int 1977
239. TMG 57
240. LBLD 115
241. HOS 195
242. Int 1977
243. Int 1977
244. Int 1977
245. SWYRA 103
246. SWYRA 104
247. HOS 219
248. HOS 223
249. LFY 32
250. FTNF 80
251. SWYRA 119
252. VI Pt 2
253. HHE 225
254. LW
255. SWYRA 162
256. LFY 72
257. LFY 72
258. FTNF 121
259. HOS 92
260. FTNF 122
261. HOS 92
262. HOS 104
263. HOS 172
264. HOS 173
265. TBNB 82
266. TMG 331
267. SWYRA 33
268. Int 1977
269. SWYRA 41
270. HHE 26

271. AISI 24
272. TMG 394
273. OHNHV
274. TMG 399
275. S1P 72
276. TMG 394
277. HW19 21
278. LFY 249
279. HHE 123
280. HHE 259
281. OHNHV
282. FTNF 121
283. OHNHV
284. HW19 21
285. Int 1977
286. LBLD 41
287. FG 77
288. FG 87
289. FG 107
290. FG 111
291. FG 113
292. FG 135
293. FG 113
294. FG 115
295. FG 166
296. FG 169
297. FG 171
298. FG 171
299. FG 199
300. FG 215
301. FG 231
302. FG 263
303. FG 267
304. FG 269
305. HOS 274
306. VI Pt 3
307. FTNF 95
308. HHE 188
309. FG 277
310. FG 307
311. FG 317
312. FG 329
313. FG 343
314. FG 343
315. FG 349

316. FG 349
317. FG 363
318. FG 373
319. AISI 172
320. TP 17
321. TP 122
322. AISI 150
323. AISI 151
324. AISI 152
325. AISI 168
326. AISI 172
327. AISI 406
328. LW
329. LWHV
330. LWHV
331. LWHV
332. LWHV
333. LWHV
334. FG 91
335. FG 127
336. FG 339
337. FG 341
338. FG 353
339. FG 355
340. FG 380
341. TP 10
342. TP 11
343. TP 17
344. TMG 221
345. VI Pt 3
346. AISI 143
347. FG 378
348. AISI 257
349. FTNF 196
350. LW
351. LW
352. LW
353. S1P 62
354. LWHV
355. LWHV
356. LWHV
357. LWHV
358. LWHV
359. LWHV
360. FTNF 106

361. location lost
362. HOS 124
363. FG 63
364. HHE 259
365. FTNF 101
366. Int 1977

ACRONYMS

AISI—As I See It
FG—The Face Game
FTNF—Face to No-Face
HHE—The Hierarchy of Heaven and Earth
HOS—Head Off Stress
HW—The Headless Way journal
Int 1977—Interview with Douglas Harding (1977)
LBLD—The Little Book of Life and Death
LFY—Look For Yourself
LW—London workshop (2000)
LWHV—Look Who's Here video (1992)
ML—Melbourne Lecture video (1991)
OHNHV—On Having No Head video (1985)
RO—Rediscovering the Obvious interview (1985)
S1P—The Science of the 1st Person
SW—Sydney workshop (1991)
SWYRA—Seeing Who You Really Are (Richard Lang)
TBNTB—To Be and Not To Be
TMG—The Trial of the Man who said he was God
TP—The Turning Point
VI—Video Interview with Douglas Harding (2001)
YT—The Yellow Toolkit

(In the References, first is the page number in Everyday Seeing, second is the acronym, and third is, where possible, the page number in the document. The books referenced are the latest editions as of the date of this book.)